A New
CREATION

6-2021

A New CREATION

From Emotional Brokenness to Spiritual Wholeness

BARBARA KABOT-VENA

XULON PRESS

Xulon Press
2301 Lucien Way #415
Maitland, FL 32751
407.339.4217
www.xulonpress.com

© 2019 by Barbara Kabot-Vena

A NEW CREATION

Most of the names of the people or person(s) written about in this book have been changed.

All rights reserved solely by the author. The author guarantees all contents are original and do not infringe upon the legal rights of any other person or work. No part of this book may be reproduced in any form without the permission of the author. The views expressed in this book are not necessarily those of the publisher.

Unless otherwise indicated, Scripture quotations taken from the New King James Version (NKJV). Copyright © 1982 by Thomas Nelson, Inc. Used by permission. All rights reserved.

Printed in the United States of America.

ISBN-13: 978-1-54566-696-8

Dedication

To my Heavenly Father,
from whom all grace, goodness, and strength abounds.

To my parents, Leslie (Lester) and Irene Kabot,
who loved me the best they knew how.

To my husband, Andy, my daughter, Sarah, and my son,
David, with whom I share unconditional love.

And to you, dear reader.
I pray you will be moved to a closer relationship
with our Lord and Savior as a result of reading this book.

ACKNOWLEDGEMENTS

I WANT TO THANK A DEAR FRIEND OF MANY YEARS, Marisa Berlinski, who believed in this book when it was just a journal and only an idea, and Lisa Owens, a close friend and co-worker, who has not only encouraged me but has faithfully labored daily in prayer for the completion and blessing of this book.

I also want to thank the pastors at my home church, Calvary Chapel of the Hudson Valley, Poughkeepsie, New York, for their genuine shepherd's love and powerful, Spirit-filled messages that taught, helped, and blessed me—Pastor Bobby Hargraves, Pastor Nick Santos, Pastor Mike Hargraves, and Pastor Matt Sweeney, as well as Pastor Bobby's wife, Liz Hargraves, for her insightful teaching, kindness, and encouragement.

A big thank you goes to my patient husband, Andy, who has had to sacrifice time with me during the many hours, spanning years, that I've worked on this book. Andy has been a constant source of strength and encouragement to me.

A special thank you to my very dear friend, AnnaLee Conti, to whom I was introduced recently by a mutual friend, and with whom I instantly became friends. AnnaLee Conti has authored four books and has worked in publishing for over forty years. She has graciously edited my manuscript free of charge, helped me navigate through the publishing industry, answered my many questions, and helped me improve my writing skills. I would have been lost without her invaluable help.

Therefore, if anyone is in Christ,
he is a new creation;

old things have passed away; behold,
all things have become new.

2 Corinthians 5:17, NKJV

Table of Contents

Part I

A Clash of Two Worlds

Part II

The Early Years

Part III

The Search for Joy and Purpose

Part IV

The Redeemed Life

Part V

The Dreaded Disease

Part I
A Clash of Two Worlds

Chapter 1

No Way Out

One dismal fall evening when I was fourteen, my parents arrived home from work to discover something they couldn't ignore. A butcher knife was dangling from the ceiling directly over my bed.

They reacted in the only sensible way they knew. Without a word, they grabbed me by both arms. Almost like two robots programmed to execute the appropriate action in a given set of circumstances, they ushered me into their Cadillac. I knew where we were headed— to New York-Presbyterian Psychiatric Hospital. Several months earlier, they'd taken my sixteen-year-old brother, Adam, there when he'd had a nervous breakdown triggered by excessive drug use.

Squished between my parents in the front seat of that opulent car, I sensed impending doom. The mingled odors of cigarette smoke and my mother's excessive perfume gagged me. No questions were asked. No words of comfort offered. No tears. Not even yelling. Nothing. The silence was so oppressive I could scarcely breathe. I felt completely alone.

Turning fourteen was supposed to be an important milestone in a girl's life. I was becoming a young lady and starting high school, yet all I felt was guilt, shame, and fear. Growing up in an emotionally abusive home, I had never received the love necessary to develop the self-confidence I needed to succeed.

As early as I can remember, I began to invent the love I needed by developing a rich fantasy life. These daydreams always had the same theme—imaginary parents who loved me and thought I was a terrific kid. My inspiration might be a friend's parents, a teacher, or characters from television, but in my dream world they loved me. I replayed these fantasies like a movie in my mind throughout the day.

The two worlds I lived in—the one in my head and the other, my real, miserable, frightening one—were so vastly different that I never confused the two. With these fantasies frequently going on in my mind, I must have appeared distracted or anti-social, but my dream life kept me content and oblivious to the horror of my loveless reality.

At school, I rarely did any work but was passed along to the next grade each year. That's what they did back then, and up until the completion of junior high school, my life remained status quo. Without warning, however, things drastically changed when I began high school. My daydreaming was now an impediment in the real world. I felt like the proverbial fish out of water. Suddenly, as life became more demanding, I could no longer manage both worlds.

Socially and emotionally, I wasn't prepared for high school. All of my friends and the other kids at school had achieved the essential social milestones, but I had never known what it meant to be praised or valued. I didn't know how to stand up for myself in the real world or how to deal successfully with my fears. Instead, I ran away from everything, even if it was only as far as my imagination.

No one knew about the other world going on in my head. I couldn't imagine telling anyone, especially not my parents. They knew nothing about the real me. How could they understand that I wasn't ready for high school?

My two worlds collided the day I started high school, culminating shortly thereafter with that drastic, unthinkable suicide attempt.

At the bus stop on my first day, the kids were all about my age, but they had something I didn't possess. For the previous fourteen years, they had lived and learned in the real world. I was just waking up from a fourteen-year daydream. I was petrified. I don't mean the natural, first-day-of-high-school jitters. I was shell-shocked, out of my element. Clearly, I didn't belong.

Growing up in the suburbs of New Rochelle, New York, I had three friends my age who lived in the neighborhood. The four of us spent every day together after school. We always hung out at my house listening to music or watching MTV. By the last year of junior high, I became closest to Debbie. As best friends, we spent more time together.

When I got off the bus on the first day at New Rochelle High, as everyone was grouping together with friends in front of the massive school waiting for the bell, I tried to hang out with Debbie. The previous year she seemed to think I was the coolest kid to be with. Now, she kept walking away from me.

Believing we were still close, I kept following her. Finally, she turned around and said, "Stop tagging behind me like a puppy dog." That shocked me. Things between us were suddenly different.

The bell rang. Somehow, I found my classroom. Typical chatter filled the room as everyone settled into their seats. I felt so out of place that I sat at my desk for less than thirty seconds before I jumped up as inconspicuously as possible and dashed out of the room. I had to get out of there.

Walking down the long, empty hallway, I saw an adult and asked, "Where's the door to get out of this place?"

Finding the door I had come in just minutes before, I exited and walked home. It was a long walk, but I didn't care. I could walk for hours as long as I had my fantasies and was safely away from that school where I didn't fit in.

When I arrived home, I discovered my parents hadn't yet left for work, so I sneaked around the side of the house to daydream happily until I heard the clatter of the electric garage door and the purr of the engine as the car pulled out. Then, I let myself in and hid out. I felt safe. There, I could daydream as much as I liked.

In the morning, I went through the motions of getting ready for school. Walking out the door, I yelled, "Bye! I'm catching the bus."

Instead of going anywhere near the bus, I again slipped around the side of the house and hid until my parents left for work. Waiting was easy. I leaned back and fell into my imaginary life where I was loved and approved of and everything was great. When they had gone, I let myself in and lay in bed. The hours felt like minutes as I fantasized the day away.

This strange new way of life continued for about a week until my friends began to wonder about my sudden, prolonged absence from school. In previous years, they had all come over to my house directly from the bus. Now, out of curiosity, they walked to my house after school and rang my doorbell. Instead of letting them in, I hid until they finally left.

Several days in a row, they rang my bell after school. I continued to hide. I felt like I was in some kind of freak show. Only to me, hiding seemed like the smartest thing to do. When my friends called me on the phone, I wouldn't answer. Running away and hiding, feeling fear and shame, and desperately trying to escape from people had now become my normal response.

After about a week, the school must have notified my parents that I was skipping school. They didn't seem surprised. They began calling home from work during the day, but I never answered.

Instead of expressing concern for what I might be going through, in the evening they mocked me. "What's the matter? Are you afraid to answer the phone?"

Either they didn't care or didn't understand that something was terribly wrong. Instead, they made me feel like I was a bad person or a failure for being too afraid to go to school. They had no clue that I was completely deficient in social skills and lacked the know-how to conduct myself with even a modicum of self-assurance in a high school setting.

No one, especially not my parents, had ever instilled in me the self-confidence I needed to face life. Even worse, they had taught me to distrust myself and everyone else. Through their words and actions, they communicated to me that I was unlovable, of no value, and should feel guilty.

About the third week of school, my friends once again came directly to my house from the bus as they'd done several times before. Only this time, they spotted me through a window. Since I'd been seen, I reasoned that I had to open the door and let them in.

"What are you doing?" they asked in shocked tones. "You're missing lots of schoolwork. We already have tons of homework."

I didn't know what to say, so I just sat there and listened, thinking there was no way I was going back to school.

Finally, I blurted out, "I'm going to kill myself."

Where did that come from? That was the first time that thought had ever entered my mind.

Unfortunately, that phrase, "I'm going to kill myself," became an evil mantra in my thinking for the next several years. That simple, yet hopeless, threat was the only power I had.

Fran, one of the three, said to me, "If touching this ashtray meant you would die instantly, would you do it?"

I thought about that for a long moment.

"Go ahead, touch it," she said. I guess she was trying to call my bluff. Even though it was just an ashtray, I couldn't touch it.

Eventually, my friends, now enlightened as to my mysterious absence, finally left. Things were different after that. I now had a self-destructive idea which had never been in my mind before. Everything was falling apart. My parents knew I was staying home from school, and my friends knew what was going on with me.

I was incapable of going back to that school, but I couldn't keep going on the way I was. Something had to change. The logical thing, I thought, was to kill myself. I cultivated that seed of an idea until it grew into something morbid.

All I had to decide was how to do it. The only means of destruction I had access to was a knife, but I knew I couldn't stab myself. So I came up with an elaborate plan. I'd tie a string to a big, sharp knife and rig it up through a large metal ring I'd tape to the ceiling over my bed. All I'd have to do was let go of the string.

Although this guillotine-like structure might have appeared dramatic, to me it just seemed to be the only logical solution to my dilemma. Long past the emotional stage, I was operating from pure logic. If I was feeling anything, I wasn't aware of it, and I certainly couldn't have communicated my feelings to anyone.

Talking to someone never entered my mind. I trusted no one—not a single person, friend, neighbor, relative, or teacher, and especially not my parents. They never talked about anything. They swept everything under the notorious rug, where it was quickly covered up, hidden away, and vehemently denied. I too had become very good at hiding bad things about myself.

But my lethal contraption didn't work the way I'd planned. The string got all tangled up, and the knife dangled ineffectively over the bed where I lay.

When my parents found my disturbing invention after arriving home from work, they knew they must act quickly, or I'd high tail it out of there. And they knew just where to take me because that's where they'd taken my brother just months before.

My brother and I were both adopted as infants from different birth families, so we had completely different genetic backgrounds from each other and from our adoptive parents (whom I will continue to refer to as my parents). Yet, neither of us were able to navigate through life without some means of escape from the pain and anguish we endured—he through drugs, and I through my fantasies. Our problems were so overwhelming that we both ended up being institutionalized during our adolescent years.

I couldn't possibly imagine what would happen at the end of this strange, silent car ride. I didn't cry. I felt nothing but emptiness.

It would be six years before I would return to the only home I knew.

Chapter 2

Away from Home

TWENTY MINUTES LATER, WE ARRIVED AT THE INFAmous New York-Presbyterian Psychiatric Hospital in White Plains, New York (New York Hospital). Set on seemingly endless grounds atop a hill, it was huge and intimidating.

Despite the quantity of buildings, we found Admissions too quickly. Its lobby was empty, dimly lit, and unwelcoming, too quiet to be a hospital. The scent of bleach mixed with pine filled the air; even the smell was unfriendly.

Led around by my parents completely against my will, I felt like a trapped prisoner. I asked to use the bathroom with the intention of either escaping through a window or somehow slipping away unnoticed. Of course, the window opening was too small.

While my dad talked to the admissions clerk, my mother watched me like a hawk. Since I was refusing to go to school and my parents had no control over me, and more particularly, due to the glaring reality that I was a danger to myself, I was admitted. Escorted by a hospital worker, I abruptly found myself locked up on one of the many units, Six North.

I was a failure. Somehow, I didn't measure up. But in spite of those feelings, I was actually glad to be there. I felt safe and, in a sense, free. Free to fantasize in order to fill the gaping void in my life and safe from the people I feared—those from my hometown who knew me, and in particular, all of my peers with whom I was evidently not up to par. I was also free from the pressures of high school and the demands of a real, normal life which I wasn't equipped to handle.

I enjoyed being at New York Hospital. It was like a country club. Unlike at home, the food was good, and everybody there was really nice to me. Also, since it was a private hospital, the furnishings and physical surroundings were elegant. The floors were all nicely carpeted, and everything was meticulously cleaned and well cared for.

On the unit, there were staff members I could talk with any time, group sessions to attend, and individual sessions with my therapist. During the day, I could play pool or ping pong or listen to the stereo in the recreation room.

Due to my suicidal status, I was confined to the unit, which encompassed two wide hallways with rooms on either side, a large sitting area for meetings, a TV area, and a recreation room. The focal point was the front office that adjoined the two hallways. They had a school on the grounds, but I wasn't allowed off the unit, and they didn't provide tutors.

Aside from my unhindered indulgence in fantasizing, to fill up my day, I played various board games or cards with any of the staff members on duty or other patients I'd decided were friendly and normal enough to interact with. Except for me, all of the patients on this unit were adults. That made the atmosphere relaxing, since I felt free from the dread of interacting with kids my own age.

From the staff members, I felt more approval and attention than at home. I even had an ongoing ping-pong competition with one of my favorite staff members who made a point of spending time with me every day he was there.

Safely tucked away in my ivory tower, I didn't have to face the outside world and all the people I dreaded. My friends called me a handful of times on the patient pay phone. Too mortified to talk to them, I quickly hung up.

Two months later, however, to my dismay, I was told that my insurance was going to run out in another month. After the customary ninety-day period of observation, it was determined that I was to return home, but that it would be best if I attended the day school program at the hospital.

Too terrified to face anyone in my hometown, that night I broke some glass on one of the window panes in my room and made a few superficial cuts around my ankle area. I had gotten that idea from a new patient I had talked with earlier that day. He had tried to reach a vein near his ankle that he believed, if severed, could be fatal. Fortunately for him, it wasn't. But he had a pretty messed up bandage, and even needed a wheelchair. As a result of my cutting incident, needless to say, the previous discharge plans had to be revised.

I was transferred to a state-run psychiatric hospital, Rockland Children's Psychiatric Center (RCPC), which could be translated "the pit of hell." In stark contrast to the country club atmosphere I'd just left, this place was dirty, uncarpeted, and could only be described as dismal. The people perfectly matched the cold atmosphere.

In my newfound misery, all I could do was cry uncontrollably and try to cut my wrist with anything sharp I could find. But no one there seemed to care that I was upset enough to try to hurt myself. They were all basically indifferent to my pain.

At this point, my life took a deep plunge into a severe, unrelenting depression. So intense was my despondency that it defied explanation. The doctor tried all types of medication to lift my gloom but to no avail. She even suggested that I be given coffee. Nothing worked. Eventually, I wound up on the maximum dose of Thorazine like everyone else there.

But I was still profoundly depressed *and*, with the medication, also a zombie. I was also unbearably tired all the time. As a child at home, I had always run around playing sports, climbing trees, playing in the woods, on the go all day. At RCPC, I didn't move. When they took us outside, I just found a place where I could lie down.

Although I hardly ate anything, I still gained weight. That was probably due to the medication that slowed down everything in my body, and because I moved around as much as a vegetable.

My crying and suicide attempts got me nowhere so I eventually stopped both. But scarcely a moment went by that I didn't say in my head, "I'm going to kill myself." That phrase, pitiful as it was, was the only comfort I had.

At RCPC, there were rules to follow, the food was absolutely disgusting, and we had chores. With no cleaning staff to vacuum, change sheets, or clean the bathrooms, as had been the case at the previous hospital, *we* were the cleaning people. And of course, we were locked up at all times. RCPC was like an institutional prison for kids.

During the first part of my stay, my parents were allowed to take me out one weekend on a four-hour pass. I spent the entire time crying uncontrollably, not really aware at the time why. My parents were confused as to why seeing them was so upsetting to me. Not knowing what I was feeling, I wasn't able to articulate anything to them. I must have wanted their compassion for my incomprehensible plight in that place.

Due to the crying, the treatment team decided not to allow any more outings or visits. I didn't see my parents for the remainder of my stay at RCPC, which was about two years. As though I were a prisoner, once a week I was brought into a room and allowed fifteen minutes to call them.

There were about twenty children together on the one unit, but we were divided into separate living quarters by gender. As though we were imbeciles, we were bossed around and yelled at about anything and everything. Maybe the staff believed that was the only way to keep us in line. Our lack of physical freedom matched the mental freedom we were allowed.

I'll never forget the two severely autistic patients who were placed with us. They rocked all day, fluttered their fingers, and had no idea who or where they were. They couldn't talk but grunted occasionally, and they were completely unaware of anyone else around them. Observing that type of person was something totally new to me. They intrigued me.

Like the walking dead, we were led through the seemingly endless halls to attend the hospital school located on the other side of the building. After school, we were taken outside for a brief time. Then, we were all put in one room to just sit and watch TV until dinner. After dinner, we did our chores, showered, and waited for our last cigarette.

We were allowed five cigarettes per day at specified times. Cigarettes were used as a means to threaten, punish, and control us. If we acted out or failed to do a chore satisfactorily, we would lose our next cigarette. That was an unbearable hardship for a smoker like me.

My older brother, Adam, had told me that I would be cool if I smoked. So, one day when I was twelve, I tried to impress him and forced myself to inhale. I enjoyed smoking and the image I believed it gave me. Once I started, it was next to impossible to stop.

When I was thirteen, my parents actually gave me permission to smoke in the house. I can't imagine what their rationale was, except that they said I was going to do it behind their back, so they might as well allow me to do it in the house. They even bought cigarettes for me when I ran out, whatever brand I asked for.

Every long, miserable day at RCPC, all I longed to do was sleep. But we were never allowed to nap. During our downtime, we were required to sit up in the plastic chairs in our common area and watch TV.

I had reached my pinnacle of despair. At age fifteen, I was incurably depressed and stuck in a mental hospital. I didn't have an inkling of hope. That bleakness was so heavy and suffocating, it literally weighed down my body, as well as my mind. My head drooped, my back was hunched, and my eyes appeared dead. I can still recall the orange bedcovers on the bed where I would lie and beg God to please just take my life.

I know God was watching over me even then in that miserable place when I felt utterly alone and forgotten. God's Word says, "When my father and my mother forsake me, then the LORD will take care of me" (Psalms 27:10). I know I had to go through what I did for a purpose. Even back then, before the day I gave my life to Him, God was keeping His promise to take care of me as His very own.

As much as I hated RCPC, it was still a mentally healthier environment than living at home with my parents. Even though the staff really had no genuine concern for the kids there, at least they were normal working people. Unlike at home where I was rewarded for being weak and demeaned and yelled at for any sign of healthy growth, at least at this place people reacted to us in normal and predictable ways. Although I wouldn't call that love, it was healthier than my home environment.

My memory of RCPC could aptly be summed up as long, boring, and debilitating. After about two years, the treatment team felt I had gotten everything I could out of my stay there, and it was time for me to move on. I was accepted into a residential treatment facility, Linden Hill, in Hawthorne, New York. Thank God, it wasn't a hospital but an actual school with nice apartments, that also had a separate building with administrative staff and therapists. Incidentally, Adam had attended this school but not as a resident. I was thankful he was no longer there.

I was more than happy to leave behind the memories of my former vegetative existence, and finally move on to something good. My depression finally began to lift, and I began to feel happier.

The living arrangements and freedom at Linden Hill were great. I felt like I had been sprung out of jail and set down in paradise. Located in a rural setting, the grounds were spacious and scenic. Unlike the RCPC treatment team, the teachers, resident counselors, and therapists genuinely cared about the kids at Linden Hill.

Since nothing was locked, we were free to come and go as we pleased and walk into town after school to the local stores. On weekends, optional outings to one of several malls nearby were usually scheduled. Most of the kids seemed nice, and I was able to make a couple of close friends.

I did well in school and became physically active again in gym class playing a lot of basketball and softball. I truly loved being there.

Although I had no genuine belief in the value of therapy, I was required to endure weekly one-hour sessions. On one occasion, to my disbelief and confusion, my therapist introduced the new concept to my thinking that my parents had played a part in causing my problems. She explained that it was unusual that Adam and I both suffered with emotional issues since we were unrelated genetically to each other or to our adoptive parents.

Having been brainwashed by my parents to think they were perfect, I blindly refused to believe they were anything but great. Of course, I wasn't aware at the time that they were hurt, bitter people putting on a façade to themselves as much as to everyone else.

Unlike most parents who admit their human shortcomings, my parents had always set themselves up on a pedestal. They had to believe they were right about everything and became defensive if anyone, particularly their kids, challenged their authority.

When I fantasized about having other parents, I always felt guilty afterwards because I believed I had betrayed my parents. It never occurred to me that they could have been the reason I needed to find love somewhere else. I had an unwavering, faithful devotion to them. In my childlike way of thinking, they were perfect—not just good parents with normal faults but faultless and great.

After three years at Linden Hill, I was able to qualify for my high school diploma. Although I'd scarcely opened a book,

I somehow had mostly Bs on my transcripts. Linden Hill had an arrangement with other high schools that although a student graduated from Linden Hill, they could receive their high school diploma from their hometown school.

At nineteen, I received my high school diploma from New Rochelle High School, though I had graced that prominent school's entranceway only twice—once on the first day of school and again running out of there a few minutes later, never to return.

Although I really enjoyed being at Linden Hill and wanted to stay longer, I was turning twenty in another month and aging out of a high school setting. During my time there, I had made some strides in feeling better about myself and learning healthy coping skills. All things considered, it was a worthwhile experience.

As my time of departure approached, the treatment team decided, without my input, what my discharge plans would entail. I was to live in a group home, called Search for Change. Back then, I only saw people in two categories—cool or loser, with no one in between. Being extremely judgmental and caring profusely how I appeared to others, I believed that a group home would be viewed as a home for the "losers" of the community. Just the name, Search for Change, made me cringe in disdain. That's how negative and hurtful my thinking was back then. Of course, no one deserves to be labeled a loser. I now believe that every human being, without exception, has innate worth, being created in the image of God (see Genesis 1:27).

In addition, the treatment team planned for me to see a therapist weekly. Again, not happening. It was further planned that I be enrolled in a training program, called VESID, which was truly the icing on the cake. That acronym stood for Vocational Educational Services for Individuals with Disabilities.

In my mind, that entire scenario was out of the question. As the person I was back then, concerned so much with the impression I made on others, the thought of being labeled as mentally ill or disabled mortified me. My biggest fear was that, in addition to the general public, people I knew would perceive me that way.

After six years of mandated treatment, I was through. From the age of fourteen, I had been forced from place to place against my will. Now that I was turning twenty, I was going to call the shots. I had had enough of hospitals, therapists, residential treatment facilities, or any other form of "treatment." I wanted to be normal.

In my young mind, I believed that if a person wasn't associated with anything treatment-related, they were normal. I believed I could achieve all of my goals on my own, and those goals were at the forefront of my mind. I wanted to have my own apartment, work at a decent job, and go to college. Being mentally ill wasn't one of my goals, and I certainly didn't think I was.

The treatment team planned for me to stay at Linden Hill for another two months or so after graduation until everything was finalized. No one asked me what I wanted to do. I wasn't allowed a say concerning my immediate future.

While I was living at Linden Hill, my father had taken me for the written test for my driver's permit and months later, for the road test. When I was eighteen, I got my driver's license, and he bought me my first car, a new Toyota Corolla.

One day while I was home on an overnight, I realized that if I wanted to be free from any and all connection to treatment, be independent and able to get on with my life, I had to break away from Linden Hill, and I needed to do it quickly and with finality. I decided I would pack up all my things and get out of that place permanently.

Without saying anything to my parents, I drove my father's car back to Linden Hill. My father always let me drive his Cadillac whenever I wanted, so that wasn't an issue. I took the Caddy so I would have the larger vehicle to move everything. Without saying a word to anyone at Linden Hill, I loaded all of my belongings into the car and drove away.

As the breeze from the open window hit my face on that beautiful fall day, I couldn't believe I'd actually moved out of there. I didn't even say goodbye to anyone. There was no one there I really trusted anyway. I was of age and could finally live my own life, free from that place and all it represented, and far away from the future they had mapped out for me, which I refused to be a part of.

I got home about thirty minutes later and proceeded to unpack. There I was at age twenty, back in my own room after being away for the past six years. I felt an inherent sense of privilege to be in my own room in my own house again. I was glad to be home.

Everything felt ostensibly the same except that I was older and felt more autonomous, but I sensed a vague emptiness, which I quickly suppressed. I was too happy being independent and away from the whole mental health scene to let anything ruin my feeling of triumph. One of my goals was now achieved, to be free from that.

My parents were surprised I'd made such a decision. I explained to them that I had had enough of that life and that I wanted to do things on my own. As I expected, they didn't agree, but they washed their hands of it the moment I got home, saying, "It's your life. Do what you want. We can't tell you what to do. You won't listen to us anyway."

I settled into the comfort of my room and began to fantasize. For the next three months, I lay in bed doing absolutely nothing but fantasizing, scarcely coming out except for meals. I had continued my dream life at Linden Hill, intermittently, but at least I was still functioning. Now, I was literally in my bed twenty-four hours a day, every day.

I guess maybe I should have gone with the treatment plan, but I wanted to be normal, and that meant severing all connections with treatment. I wanted what everyone else wanted out of life—to get my own place, go to college, and get a good job.

I had very distinct goals and was set on accomplishing them, but my fantasies took priority. It was just too easy to procrastinate. I was, for all intents and purposes, immobilized, happy in my dreamlife, yet at the same time, depressed in the real life.

I became a freak again, an enigma—emerging briefly from hiding daily, not wanting to, but needing food. We weren't allowed to eat in our room. Being so zoned out, I was too stupid to disobey. Embarrassed and afraid some of Adam's friends might be around, I'd force myself to enter the kitchen. From all that obsessive daydreaming, I felt hung over as though I'd spent days of drugging and drinking. Like some monster, I'd get food, eat it as fast as I could, and return to my dark lair.

This went on for three straight months until, to my amazement, something happened one disturbing evening that not only got me out of bed but also out of that house and into my own place *in one night!*

And thank God it did. It was my turning point.

Chapter 3

The Turning Point

THAT EVENING, TAKING A BREAK FROM MY USUAL fantasy binge, I went into the kitchen at about 11:00 p.m. The house was quiet. My mother, always the proverbial night owl, was still up and about. As she busied herself organizing things, I began to talk with her.

We weren't discussing anything in particular, but we got into an argument. I can't remember what it was about. Suddenly, out of nowhere, she began to mimic everything I said. Although obviously childish, it was calculated to frustrate and taunt me as though she was trying to gain power over me—like a game she wanted to win.

Her guard was down, and her façade lifted. For the first time, I finally began to realize that she wasn't the perfect, loving mother I'd always believed her to be. She was acting hurtful and uncompassionate. During the past three months, she hadn't once come into my room to see if I was okay or to offer a single word of comfort. I didn't understand until years later that she didn't know how to love. At the time, I didn't know that she was also hurting and sorrowful to such an extent that she simply didn't have it in her to reach out to me in my time of need.

Until the age of twenty, having been overwhelmed with guilt for years, I blamed myself for all of my problems, believing I was a failure and had let my parents down. I was convinced *I* was the cause of all my problems.

Having been conditioned to believe my parents were all-knowing and benevolent about everything, I could only put them up on a pedestal. After all those years of my father yelling at me for something stupid he thought I'd done, I hadn't understood that his actions weren't normal. I believed my messing up had caused him to yell.

Until that night, I loved my parents in an excessive, unhealthy way. I had often prayed they wouldn't die because I feared I'd be lost without them. It never occurred to me that they had something to do with what I was going through. They were so good at convincing me they were perfect I believed it hook, line, and sinker. As a result of being infused with their insecurities and their need for *me* to be the sick one, I had been unable to challenge them.

Unable to even feel anything, let alone express anger, I had been locked up in my own guilt like a prisoner. I was immobilized by fear of people, unable to defend myself or speak up for myself to anyone. Without a shred of confidence, I was convinced I was a bad person.

Now, a new concept entered my mind. Suddenly, I understood that I had fantasized about other parents because mine hadn't met my basic needs. All those years of failure, depression, fear, and suicidal thoughts hadn't been my fault. That knowledge set me free!

This awakening was the catalyst to spur me on to bigger and better things. In that instant, all of my immobilizing guilt turned into empowering rage. For the first time, I could feel anger. With this new epiphany, I switched from blaming myself to blaming my parents.

Of course, this black-and-white thinking wasn't good either. It wasn't until years later that I came to realize that, although my parents' fear and anger caused a lot of damage, no one is ever entirely to blame. Adam and I were merely victims of victims. Our parents had suffered severe hardships during their own formative years.

Too angry and young to appreciate those realities, I shouted, "It's *your* fault I have problems. *You* guys caused Adam's and my problems."

This ruckus roused my father, who joined my mother in the argument. Challenging them only made them defensive. I tried to reason with them, to make them see the truth, but they were not open to discussion.

They fervently justified themselves, saying I was the one with all the problems. Asserting that they were happy with their life and with the way they were, they declared they didn't need to change. I was the one who needed to change. That became their new slogan.

They simply weren't able or willing to accept any blame. They maintained a guilt-free conscience at all costs, asserting that they had done nothing wrong.

I realized they would never be willing to admit they were wrong about anything. I was and always would be their enemy, no matter what I did.

I was no longer the weak automaton they could easily control, though. Regrettably, at this period of my life, I was so angry with them that it seethed out of my every pore. They were on the defensive, claiming their innocence, and I was now the mean, ungrateful one. I desperately needed an exit plan.

Although I didn't know God at this time, He was clearly working behind the scenes. A few months prior, Adam had been engaged to be married. He was living with his fiancée in an apartment in Mt. Vernon, New York, one town over from our house in New Rochelle. One night, he had another nervous breakdown and was rushed by ambulance to the hospital.

While Adam was receiving treatment at St. Vincent's Hospital, his fiancée had gone back home to live with her family. They never married, leaving my father paying the rent each month on a two-year lease for an empty apartment.

Either my dad decided to call my bluff and challenge me, or he just wanted to get me out of the house because he couldn't handle my accusations, I can't be sure, but it was probably a little of both. He yelled in his usual mode of speech, "If you hate us so much and want to get away from us so badly, then why don't you take Adam's apartment? It's yours. I'm stuck paying the rent on an empty apartment. Just move there. Go!"

I think he assumed I wouldn't leave. But I sure didn't have to think twice about that offer. Infused with rage toward them, I was energized with a strength and purpose I'd never known before.

I quickly packed all my things. That same night, I moved into that apartment and was out on my own. That sounds too good to be true, but only God could have worked out that speedy exodus.

This one-bedroom apartment, completely furnished and decorated attractively, was now mine. Adam didn't care. I don't think he wanted the responsibility of an apartment. Some months later, he was happy to move back home into the lap of luxury.

I was thrilled to have my own place. With my new-found hatred for my parents replacing the former blind love, living with them wouldn't have been good. Although my anger and hatred toward them was obviously wrong, going from one extreme to the other seemed to have a temporary purpose at the time, which was to get me out of that unhealthy environment.

Seeing my parents fall from their pedestal of perfection and realizing my problems weren't all my fault was liberating. But if they had caused much of what I'd suffered, I had to understand how and why it happened.

What negative influence could have had such a destructive effect on me and my brother? Why were they so defensive? What dark secret were they desperately trying to hide about themselves?

Part II
The Early Years

Chapter 4

Seeds of Fear and Harbored Emotions

When I was little and spoke and acted funny like the young child I was, my father used to make fun of me. Seemingly for his own entertainment, truly not understanding its impact on a little girl, he laughed at my expense and teased me until I got upset and threatened to run away. Then he would mimic the way I said "run away." I guess it sounded funny coming from the mouth of a three-year-old. Knowing I was too young and afraid to actually go anywhere, he would then say, his tone dripping with sarcasm, "Go ahead. Good-bye. See ya." (Our housekeeper told me about this years later.)

Whether saying it outright or by implication, my father called me stupid every day of my life. He criticized just about everything I said or did. Needless to say, that had a profound effect on me. His demeaning words destroyed my ability to believe in myself as an intelligent person. For many years, I believed I was stupid.

To say I had an inferiority complex didn't even come close to scratching the surface of the effect that man had on me. Not able to be my true self, I became deeply depressed throughout my childhood and teenage years as a constant battle raged within my heart and mind to be the intelligent person I knew I was but was too afraid to be.

Of course, as a child, I had no comprehension that all of this was going on under the surface. I loved my father. Since I was so young when I was yelled at and made to feel stupid, I thought that was normal. I was eager for my father's approval, but the more I tried to win him over by my acts of kindness or displays of talent or intelligence, the more he put me down verbally and criticized everything I did. Of course, I felt crushed and rejected, but I didn't stop trying to win his approval.

One day when I was about ten, I set out to clean the garage, which was a mess from years of neglect. Things that had never been thrown out had just continued to pile up over time. He'd always complained about what a mess it was and how he couldn't stand it. I was sure doing this job would definitely impress him.

I spent hours on that garage, cleaning and organizing. Then, with great anticipation, I called him to come to the garage to see what I'd done. He wasn't very eager, but after my coaxing, he finally agreed to take a look.

"What the hell's the matter with you?" he yelled bitterly. "I didn't want you to do this. You should have left it alone."

I was crushed. But more than that, I was perplexed. Why would he react that way when my motive was to please him?

What I hadn't realized at the time was that he was actually embarrassed by his mess and that was why he had complained about it so many times. He was trying to make it clear that he was aware of the glaring clutter and thus not appear to us or others as ignorant of the problem. His pride was further injured by the fact that I was the one who had cleaned it up. As a result of his feelings of chagrin, he wasn't able to show gratitude for my genuine act of love for him. He could only express hostility.

Perhaps, having grown up with so little during the Depression, he couldn't bear to throw anything away, even if it was just useless junk. His anger must have gone deeper than a mere annoyance about his things. Maybe it wasn't just about his belongings. Maybe I had unearthed something else intangible, long since buried, secretly hidden—maybe his own feelings of inferiority.

It could be that for years he'd been trying to bury emotional pain that he wasn't able to bring to the surface but continued to sweep out of sight lest anyone notice. At the time, of course, I couldn't possibly have understood all that.

On the surface, he seemed like an angry tyrant, but below the livid display and hard-shelled exterior, he was always protecting his fragile self-image at all costs. What shame was he trying to hide?

By the time I was about seven, I was essentially programmed to be dumb. There was the "stupid me" I displayed to the world, and the "real me" I knew was buried somewhere deep inside. The real me was intelligent, joyful, and confident, but during my childhood and adolescence, I lived within the confines of the stupid me. Everyone only knew the stupid me. I never, or rarely ever, got to be the real me.

In a rare moment, I was able to hear what was going on in my thinking underlying everything that played out on the surface. Like a recording, I heard my own voice say, "You're supposed to be stupid." That was how I was programmed. Consequently, I was plagued every waking hour with the fear of becoming brain damaged.

I spent almost every moment of my young life fighting off the persistent fear that somehow my brain had been adversely affected by something. I believed that certain things could actually cause brain damage. For example, if there was a speck of something odd in my food or if I walked by a truck and accidentally breathed in fumes, I believed I would instantly have a mental defect causing me to be stupid. Those worries consumed me.

These fearful attacks bombarded me continually. Incapable of fighting them off, I would quickly succumb to the belief that

I was truly brain damaged and would live in a stupor, controlled by fright and gloom. When I looked back on a previous fear, I would realize how foolish it was, but in the trenches of it, it was real and believable. It felt like I was fighting for my life.

Eventually, after several hours of captivity to dread and worry, one particular fear would wear off, and I'd be free to be myself again for a brief time. But the new feelings of freedom and happiness never lasted long. The fears always returned.

Depression would once again overwhelm me, as I continued to subsist without any hope. The real me only lasted maybe an hour or less, or at the very most on a rare occasion, half a day. I'd be free only until the next fear pursued me, and the fight continued. And I always lost.

Of course, none of those fears were based in reality. But I *believed* my fear was real, that I had truly suffered brain damage caused by one ludicrous thing or another. And that caused me to be profoundly depressed and immobilized. It's not that I was actually an unintelligent child, but feeling so overwhelmingly defeated and utterly hopeless, I was preoccupied and distracted with worry to the point of not being able to focus on anything else. Of course, in such a daze, I appeared stupid to everyone else.

All I knew was that I had to be careful because anything around me could give me brain damage. That was a miserable way to exist. Throughout my entire childhood and teenage years, I was semiconscious, withdrawn, and lifeless. Socially, I was unemotional and vaguely responsive, like a zombie, bewildered and awash with fear. I knew the real me existed, but she was trapped inside. Yet, I never stopped believing that the real me was there and that one day I would be completely well and successful.

I wonder how many young people today are plagued in some way with not being able to be the real person they know is buried somewhere inside of them but for some reason is not able to emerge and show the great beauty hidden within. When God looks at every one of us, He sees the beauty inside.

According to Isaiah 64:8 and Jeremiah 18:4-6, God, the Master Potter, remolds us into something beautiful when we yield our lives to Him. And Ecclesiastes 3:11 declares, "He has made everything beautiful in its time."

I continually asked my mother if this thing or that caused brain damage. Oblivious to my plight, she never expressed any concern about what I seemed to be going through or curiosity as to why I was recurrently asking these questions. She would usually just answer my inquiries in a relatively pleasant and logical way. Sometimes she'd get fed up with my persistence and sigh in exasperation at how ridiculous my questions sounded. When she became too annoyed by my need for reassurance, she would refuse to answer. Like my father, she too was very critical and condemning.

At the time, naturally, I was unaware that my fears came directly from my parents' unconscious fear of my intellectual and emotional growth. For whatever reason, they didn't want me to be the intelligent, self-confident, happy girl I could be. Despite how much I wanted to be the person I knew I could be, the person my parents molded me to be had full control, and I lived within those constraints.

Why were they so fearful? Why were they so desperate to protect their self-images, even to the extent of lashing out at their children?

Chapter 5

THEY PREFERRED DARKNESS

MY DAD, LESLIE (EVERYONE CALLED HIM LES OR Lester), grew up during the Depression. Being the eldest child and without a father in the home, he had to quit high school in order to find work to provide for his mother and younger brother and sister.

He had nothing when he married my mom. With some of her money, which she'd saved through years of working, he started his own printing business, a trade he'd learned from an uncle. After several years of ruthlessly pounding the pavement to drum up business, not accepting no for an answer, he made his print shop a success.

From sparse beginnings, his business soon filled a corner on East Gunhill Road in the Bronx, New York, employing about twelve people, including a full-time artist. Among its many features, his print shop held several large printing presses, machinery for packaging, a dark room, an employee lounge, and a large front office. As the boss he, naturally, set his own hours and chose to work Monday through Friday.

Like clockwork, he got up around seven in the morning to head out to work at about eight, and he was always home by five, which was an hour or two before dinner was actually ready and put on the table. He never worked on weekends. Being the breadwinner of the family and old-school in his thinking, he didn't want his wife to have to work. Years later, though, Mom did eventually work part time in his office to help out, by choice not necessity.

My dad was able to overcome his poverty and become financially successful. Material things, though, seemed to hold a deeper meaning for him, something I could never understand. He always purchased the newest Cadillac every two years. Maybe he was trying to say something—maybe not to others but to himself.

Dad often took my friends and me places, dropping us off and picking us up from bowling, horseback riding, or the mall. He often took me with him on his weekend errands. Whenever he asked me to go, I rarely said no.

Despite his criticism of me, I couldn't help but admire him. It was so easy for him to talk to people, even to a total stranger. He had a way with people and could strike up a conversation with anyone, but it was never too involved or boring—just small talk or something lighthearted. He had a witty sense of humor and could easily make people laugh. I admired that.

I enjoyed our weekly trips to the bagel shop in town. Driving back, he always took out a salted bagel, still hot, and split it with me to eat on the way home. That is a good memory.

When I was about seven, we were driving somewhere in the city on an errand for his business and I noticed a sign posted in front of a store that said, "Free kittens." Of course, I began asking him unceasingly to go back so I could get one. Despite the fact that he said Mom was going to be furious if he brought home a kitten, he couldn't say no in that father-daughter moment.

But there was a dark side to him as well, even in social settings. If something angered him, and something usually did on a daily basis, he would curse and yell in an angry, self-righteous tirade. If he perceived that someone treated him unfairly or inconsiderately, a quarrel was sure to ensue. He would often get into intense arguments with the grocery store cashier when he thought he was being overcharged, even if it was just a matter of fifty cents. Angrily, he would walk off grumbling that he'd been unfairly treated as if deeply wounded. He was a verbal fighter, a big-time yeller. Nobody liked to be the brunt of his anger.

Aside from the daily arguments, the bottom line with my dad was that he was always on the alert not to look stupid, even if it meant making everyone else look stupid first. He was known to go after his employees in his print shop on a regular basis for something stupid he believed they'd done, or he'd get angry over the idiocy of a business associate whom he believed had done something backhanded to him. Then, in the sanctity of his glassed-in front office, he would rant and rave and turn red in the face in a hailstorm of curses until the tempest would finally blow over some twenty minutes later.

My mother, Irene, also grew up in the Depression. The middle child and only girl, she lost the father she adored in a car accident when she was very young and was stuck with her mother, whom she described as very mean and physically abusive.

Unlike my dad, who had a natural gift for socializing, my mom had a more difficult time conversing with others. It didn't come naturally to her. She was often misunderstood. Although very intelligent, well-read, and well-spoken, she was more of a thinker than a schmoozer. She wasn't the emotional type. Expressing her feelings never seemed to go well.

I recall on one occasion she was upset about something and angry enough to want to express it to my dad. She went into the bathroom and dripped water into her eyes so it looked like she was crying, but he was probably on to her.

My mother never loved my father. When they first met, he fell in love with her immediately. He knew she was the one. He pursued her, but she repeatedly told him that she didn't love him and just wanted to be friends. He didn't care. He told her many times he would marry her anyway. After six years of this dating-as-friends scenario, my mother finally agreed to marry him. She was getting on in years and had grown up in a time when it was financially and socially prudent to be married. Still, she made it clear that she was not in love with him.

This fact never seemed strange to me growing up, but years later, I had to wonder why my father had been willing to commit himself to someone who didn't love him. How melancholy that wedding day must have been for my mother—that big day that was supposed to be so special and intimate. How disappointing it must have felt for her to say "I do," uniting herself to a man she didn't love. She must have wondered if she was making a big mistake. Perhaps, she thought if she had held out just a little longer for true love, she might have found it.

Maybe throughout the years, deep down, she thought that life had dealt her an unfair hand. Those were things she never confided in me. She would never admit to anyone her true feelings if it put her in an unfavorable light.

Casually, devoid of any emotion, was how she told me the fact that she never loved Dad. She explained that he just wasn't the one. Not seeming embarrassed or self-conscious, she just stated it as a commonly accepted fact.

My dad knew how it was. She'd discussed this long-held fact with equal abandon whether at home or at dinner at a restaurant. How must he have felt spending his entire life with someone who often declared she didn't love him?

"Back in our day," she'd say, "the reality was that a woman needed to be married." My dad would just sit there not seeming the slightest bit upset or annoyed.

Sadly, my mom didn't understand that love is more than a passionate feeling. I've learned that love is actually a decision. Over the years, I've come to understand that love is a daily, continual commitment to honor, to take actions of kindness toward the other person, to encourage, and to take care of the other person. I've realized for love to be real or to mean anything, it requires daily sacrificial actions in the other person's best interest.

By God's grace, I learned how to love in my marriage because of the clarity of what the Bible teaches and due to my commitment to doing what pleases God. It didn't happen overnight, but over time with His help, I grew more loving. God's Word defines love this way:

> Love suffers long and is kind; love does not envy; love does not parade itself, is not puffed up; does not behave rudely, does not seek its own, is not provoked, thinks no evil; does not rejoice in iniquity, but rejoices in the truth; bears all things, believes all things, hopes all things, endures all things (1 Corinthians 13:4-7).

In order to fit in and be accepted by their peers in their newfound sphere of wealth and status, my parents needed to have children. Like all the other Jewish families in their affluent suburban neighborhood, along with membership in one of the two local synagogues, children were an important blessing. Without them, in this community, my parents fell short.

Despite my mother's lack of physical attraction to my dad, they apparently tried for several years to have their own but to no avail. They wanted a boy and a girl. To achieve another rung on their ladder of success, they went to great lengths to acquire us. They adopted Adam and me as infants from separate families—Adam in New York and me in Los Angeles, California, three years later.

All I know about my biological mother is that she was still in high school and living at home with her own parents when she got pregnant. My parents told me she was Jewish but that they knew nothing about my biological father. Apparently, since she was too young and unprepared to provide for me, her parents urged her to put me up for adoption so I could have a good home.

When my parents heard of a Jewish baby becoming available, they practically jumped through hoops to adopt me. They had to fly out to California from New York, and then stay at a hotel with Adam, my soon-to-be brother, who was three at the time.

Their stay was prolonged because I was born prematurely and needed an incubator, along with an extended stay at the hospital. They wound up having to pay not only the adoption agency, but also for their long hotel stay, the hospital bill, and the airfare. In addition, my dad had to take off work that length of time.

In spite of the many hurdles, my adoptive parents were able to get what they wanted, a boy and a girl. Because they cared deeply what others thought of them, they had acted determinedly on their strong need to fit in. Just as being single in their day could be socially intolerable and embarrassing, being a childless couple carried its own haunting stigma. Now, they could feel equal to their neighborhood peers. They had married for the wrong reasons and followed suit by adopting children for the wrong reasons.

My parents seemed to live by a unique code of ethics, which was probably influenced more by their own personal life experiences than by the generation in which they grew up. For example, according to their standards, it was okay to lie if you had to.

When they finally realized that to be parents they had to adopt, my mother, being older than her husband and afraid she might be too old to be allowed to adopt, lied about her age. To this day, her incorrect age, forty-six, is on my birth certificate. She never once told me that lying about her age was wrong. I don't think it ever crossed her mind that it might be morally wrong to lie in order to complete the legalities of adoption.

I recall one day when I was about ten sitting with my mother in the office of a home insurance salesman. One of the questions he asked was what material our house was constructed of. She told him it was brick, even though our house was made of wood. Since a brick house is less flammable than wood, we could get a reduction on our insurance cost. I spoke up and told the man our house was made of wood. My mother laughed at my naivety and explained to me later that we got a better deal by answering her way.

One of my dad's primary aims in life was to give my mom a good life. She loved to travel, so my father made a point of taking her on numerous vacations to various beautiful places around the world. In fact, they traveled extensively before adopting Adam and me. Then, during their parenting years, they continued to travel, leaving us home with a babysitter.

My mother didn't like to drive. Without fail, Dad chauffeured her every Saturday to the beauty salon to get her hair and nails done. He would drop her off and then wait at home on the couch watching TV shows, such as John Wayne westerns, until he got a call from her that she was ready to be picked up.

Each week, she would give him a list and off he would go to do the weekly grocery shopping. Sometimes they did the shopping together, but he preferred to go alone for the sake of expediency. She could get obsessive in the grocery store and deliberate over each and every item.

In essence, she had a life of leisure. Having grown up in abject poverty, after getting married, and after my dad's business became a success, my mother truly wanted for nothing materially. She had just about every store and major credit card, a beautiful house, a nice car, a cleaning lady who did all the housework, and a devoted husband who loved her.

In addition to the many years of extensive travel, Dad took her out often to the opera, to Broadway shows, and to nice restaurants. They entertained regularly and were part of a bowling league. While she played Mahjong weekly with the neighborhood ladies, he played poker with the men. During their many outings when we were young, we had the dreaded babysitter, Mrs. Mal, an impassive, very old lady.

Although my mom had what seemed to be a great, comfortable life, she wasn't happy. I could see in her eyes her dissatisfaction with life. She clearly longed for something more. Maybe she privately dreamed of a different life. She took great pride in her intelligence, and I know she believed she could have done so much more with her life if given the chance to go to college and establish a career.

More than once, my mom shared with me, with clear resentment in her tone, that she had wanted to go to college but never had the money. The little money her mother could eventually scrape together went to her two brothers for college, with no consideration for my mom's ambitions. Her older brother, my uncle Jesse, became a pharmacist; her younger brother, my uncle Arnold, a college professor.

Undoubtedly, my mom aspired to being more than a mother and a housewife, or even working in my dad's print shop. It's not a stretch to see that my dad was not worldly or educated enough for her. He was a simple guy, a people person, with a coarse, down-to-earth way about him.

Throughout the years, as I observed my mother's apparent dissatisfaction with life, I vowed to myself that no matter what, I would never marry a man unless I truly loved him. That oath served me well, and I was later to marry the man of my dreams.

Unfortunately, my parents didn't have loving childhoods. Coming from harsh upbringings, with histories they desperately wanted to bury, they cared for and related to each other and to their children the best they knew how.

Despite their best intentions, their home was fraught with mental anguish and pain. Instead of love, there were guilt trips. Instead of teaching, name calling. The household was anything but a nurturing environment.

Instead of looking inward to try to become better people than those they learned from growing up, and instead of being thankful for all of their blessings, they allowed their pasts and insecurities to control them and make them angry and bitter. Embracing a victim mentality, their tendency toward self-protection caused them to react in defensive and hurtful ways.

They simply needed to admit their human short-comings and find healing. No one is perfect, but my parents mistakenly needed to believe they were. If only they could have known and accepted the truth that we are all sinners and that there is a God who accepts and loves us anyway, they could have found forgiveness and healing.

But they preferred to deny the truth and remain in darkness. Refusing to accept any responsibility for their actions, they covered up their guilt. In John 3:19-21, Jesus said that people do not come into the light of truth because they love their sin. They prefer the dark so they can hide their wrong-doing. As a result, they never get the healing they need.

> And this is the condemnation, that the light has come into the world, and men loved darkness rather than light, because their deeds were evil. For everyone practicing evil hates the light and does not come to the light, lest his deeds should be exposed. But he who does the truth comes to the light, that his deeds may be clearly seen, that they have been done in God (John 3:19-21).

Although my parents navigated through the complex task of childrearing, no doubt, with the best of intentions, they provided no parameters and no order. We were made to feel guilty but were never punished. Even our feelings were considered wrong and quickly suppressed. All of this resulted in a loss of love and a travesty of childhood.

Chapter 6

No Boundaries

MATERIALLY, OUR PARENTS PROVIDED FOR US WELL. Despite their impoverished beginnings, they were able to provide for us the good things they never had. We had a nice house and plenty of food, clothes, and toys.

Our emotional needs were not as well accounted for. My parents simply didn't understand that there was substantially more to love than providing for their children's physical needs and giving their children what they wanted materially. Caring and affection weren't part of the deal. It just wasn't in their skill set.

Although we got everything we wanted, a guilt trip was always attached. When I was young, all of my friends had leather Adidas, the white ones with the three black stripes on the sides. They cost a hundred dollars at the time, but my friends had them, and I had to have them.

Of course, I got the sneakers. My parents could never say no. But in order to get them, I had to endure the story of how all they had to wear on their feet at my age was a piece of cardboard held together with string and how I was lucky to have such a nice pair of sneakers when they never had the luxuries that I took for granted.

I feel genuine empathy that they had to struggle for the basic needs of life, and for all the people who suffered through or were affected by the Depression, but as children we didn't have the capacity to relate to that nor understand it when it was presented to us in the context of a guilt trip.

Drilled into my head with every material thing I received was the message that I didn't deserve it. A bike, a radio, clothes, a stuffed animal—all came with culpability heaped on top. Even as we ate a meal, my father reminded us that when he was a child, his family couldn't afford meat so he had to eat mustard sandwiches.

I don't think they purposely meant to make us feel bad, but those incessant guilt trips had a lingering effect on me that even many years later reared its ugly head whenever I bought something for myself, even if it was only a five-dollar hairbrush. It took many years to finally be able to enjoy receiving a gift or to take pleasure in buying myself something nice without feeling uneasy or hesitant.

There were no boundaries or limits in our home. We were expected to take care of our own needs. My brother and I had free rein to do as we pleased. We came and went without being held accountable. Our dad would wake us up in the morning for school, but then he went off to work shortly after. No one was around to make us breakfast. My mother slept in until about noon. And that's not because she had a night job. She didn't work until years later.

We got dressed, helped ourselves to a bowl of cereal, and got ourselves on the bus. Back in those days, children didn't need constant supervision as they do today. I remember walking alone several blocks to my elementary school.

When Adam was thirteen, he began smoking pot in his room, and my parents were completely powerless to stop him. They refused to accept that reality until years later when his pot smoking was just too blatant to ignore.

Over the next several years, he progressed to doing other drugs. Then, they unwaveringly refused to believe that he was doing anything other than *just* pot. They simply had no control over him.

I started smoking cigarettes at twelve years of age for the sole purpose of impressing my older brother. As I mentioned earlier, my parents gave me permission to smoke in the house and actually bought me cigarettes. They knew I was going to do it anyway, they explained, so they might as well allow it so I wouldn't have to sneak around. They seemed to want to be the cool parents. Instead of enforcing rules, they wanted to gain our acceptance, more like they were our friends than our parents.

Since they couldn't control us, we were never punished. If we did something wrong, they would condemn us verbally rather than address the behavior. They didn't distinguish between us as persons and the behavior we displayed. If we had a fight with a neighborhood kid, for example, they said we were mean and bad. It wasn't our behavior that was bad; *we* were bad. Maybe they were afraid if they tried to punish us, we wouldn't listen, or we would get angry and hate them.

When I was about ten, I went out one day with a group of friends. We walked to the nearby shopping center, and I stole some candy from a store. At some point after we got back to my house, my mother found out and confiscated the brown bag of candy, making it clear that stealing was wrong. But about ten minutes later, she gave all of the candy back to me, explaining, "It's already done. You might as well have it." That was the closest she ever came to intervening in a disciplinary way with me.

I recall thinking how wonderful she was to give me back the candy. Maybe that was what she wanted me to think. Either that or she truly didn't know the right way to handle the situation.

I believe the way they treated us was motivated by good intentions. Even when they told me how wrong my feelings were and how I *should* feel, I fully believe they were genuinely trying to impart to me their lifelong wisdom and didn't understand the impact of their criticism. They thought they were being helpful whenever they scrutinized my feelings. Nonetheless, their actions took a destructive toll on me.

In the same way that my intelligence, my joy, and my social skills were extinguished, my emotions were also snuffed out. My feelings were never just accepted for what they were—mine, and therefore, valid. Instead, I was taught that my feelings were wrong and needed to be corrected or were too foolish to have at all.

One time when I was about four, we were visiting friends who had a large dog. Apparently, he was very friendly, but that dog was twice my size. I was reasonably afraid of it. Every time it came into the room, I'd run in fear.

My parents just couldn't believe that I was afraid of such an obviously friendly dog. Instead of reassuring me by acknowledging my fear with a few sympathetic words of understanding and explaining to me that the dog was friendly, they yelled at me for being frightened. They wanted to make it clear to me how foolish my fear was since the dog was so clearly harmless. They didn't know how to accept my feelings and take the time to gradually acclimate me to the dog. They truly believed they were helping me by putting me down.

To my parents, being right was more important than being compassionate. They had to be right about everything, and we were always wrong. After all, how could young, inexperienced kids ever know more than older, more experienced adults?

One morning when I was about seven, I woke up to find that I was covered with red dots all over my face, arms, and legs. At the time, I had no idea it was the chicken pox (or measles or whatever it might have been). I was frightened and immediately sought out my mother for comfort. I found her in bed.

I came to her clearly upset and frightened. After looking me over, she lay back in her bed and laughed heartily. I was confused and tried to understand. Finally, she said, "Silly, this is good news. You have the chicken pox. Now that you've got it, you won't ever get it again. This is great."

She wasn't concerned about my fear and worry, only about getting her point across that I should be glad I got the chicken pox early in life to get it out of the way. Once again, it was all about feeling the "right" way. My feelings were summarily dismissed as silly. To her, it wasn't about showing tenderness or compassion; it was always about being right.

Without the acceptance to freely express my feelings, I learned early on not to trust my emotions. As a result, even as a young child, I began to rely on logic rather than feelings. My passion for life and emotional expression diminished. I learned to be lifeless and cold, like my mother. She was a logical thinker. In fact, she appeared to be thinking all the time. She didn't seem to know how to express emotions. Whenever she tried, it usually came out wrong.

As a child and teenager, I was plagued by yet another debilitating worry—what people thought of me, another trait I got from my mother, who was wrapped up in herself and how she came across to others. She cared profusely what others thought of her.

On several occasions, I expressed to my parents my worry about what someone might think of me in a particular situation. They called that ridiculous and constantly drilled into my head that I was wrong to worry about what anyone thought of me, and they quickly became annoyed whenever I did. To care what anyone thought of me, they repeatedly told me, was the most foolish and weakest thing a person could do. It probably hadn't dawned on them that I was just a child.

One day, my mother wanted me to put some old bread out by the side of our house to feed the birds. I didn't want to because the bread was so old it was green. She never could bear to throw anything away. I didn't want the neighbors to see me with that weird-looking bread. Instead of respecting the way I felt, my mother got upset and admonished me for being so foolish as to care what anyone thought. In spite of how I felt, she forced me to go out there with that ghastly bread.

My father was especially adamant in his thinking that you should never care what anyone thought of you. He often asserted, with deep pride in his voice, "I couldn't care less what people think of me."

With exasperated sighs, they'd often ask me, "Why do you care? Who cares what they think?" That was their theme whenever my concern about what someone might think of me came up and, of course, it came up a lot.

They managed to convince me that my caring was foolish and dead wrong and that I needed to stop caring. But how was I supposed to feel one way and make myself believe I felt just the opposite? It was my job to learn how to lie to myself. I was supposed to not care even when I did.

Consequently, *another* battle constantly raged inside me. For many years, whenever I *did* care what someone thought of me, I would tell myself over and over that I didn't. Trying so hard not to care, brainwashed to believe caring was wrong, I would tell myself repeatedly, "I don't care what anyone thinks of me. It doesn't matter." But of course, that was a lie. Deep down I really did care, even to an unhealthy extent.

Now, I naturally *care* what people think of me in the general sense, but I never *worry* about it. Since I live to please God only, and I am kind toward others as He commands, there is nothing whatsoever to worry about. It's all about Him, not me.

Although their actions seemed cruel, my parents simply didn't possess essential elements of love to give. If a bucket is empty, a person can't reach into it, take something out, and give it to another person. How could I blame them for not giving to me what they didn't possess?

I was angry with them for a long time. After I gave my life over to God many years later, I realized that not to forgive them would be sin. God commands us to forgive others. He is clear in His Word that if we don't forgive others, He will not forgive us (Matthew 6:15). God enabled me to genuinely forgive my parents.

According to Romans 8:28, God is in control of all things, and He has a reason for everything He allows in a person's life, even a painful upbringing. He is my loving Heavenly Father who fills me with all the love I need.

After what I dubbed my "turning point" at age twenty when I finally saw my parents differently, I was blessed with the opportunity to move into my own apartment. Coming to an understanding of what had happened to me, I was eager to put my past aside and move on. I proceeded on with the business of achieving my goals *my* way. I pursued finding a job and going to school.

In the midst of these activities, though, I couldn't help but feel a lack of meaning and purpose in my life. I wasn't depressed. I was quite happy with the direction my life was going. Instead, I felt a profound dissatisfaction with life, no matter what good things might have happened on a particular day. I longed for *real* joy, not just fleeting moments of happiness that would always fade away the next day.

This unmistakable void in my soul was something I needed to fill. I had to know if there was anything more to life than this sense of mundane futility with no purpose or meaning.

Speaking through the prophet Jeremiah, God says in His Word, "And you will seek Me and find Me, when you search for Me with all your heart" (29:13). As human beings created in the image of God, we all have souls that yearn for spiritual fulfillment, purpose, and answers about eternal matters. The Bible teaches that God created us that way and that everyone has a God-shaped void in their heart that only He can fill. People may suppress or deny those spiritual longings, but they are still there.

Ecclesiastes 3:11 speaks of how God has instilled into each of us a strong desire for spiritual fulfillment and eternal answers. That is why we have a distinct inability to be fully satisfied with earthly pleasures and pursuits.

Not knowing God at this time, and being as far away from Him as I could possibly be, I spent the next ten years on a relentless quest to fill my pervasive emptiness.

Although this resolve took me to some painful, strange, and even dangerous places, I wouldn't stop until I found the truth that would answer my pressing questions: Why am I here? Is this life all there is? Is there something that can fill me with hope and enduring joy?

Part III
The Search for Joy and Purpose

Chapter 7

Financially Attached

More than anything, I wanted to live a normal life and pursue my goals completely on my own. I knew in my heart that as long as I was connected in any way to my parents, I'd never be free. I had to sever all ties with them. The only remaining one was monetary, but it was the most difficult to break.

Being financially independent from my parents seemed next to impossible to achieve. Every month, my dad wrote out checks for all of my bills, just as he'd done for Adam. In order to no longer have to associate with them, that had to stop. My well-being depended on it.

Financial independence became one of my main focuses. In the newspaper's classified section, I found quite a few jobs I actually qualified for—ones that said "no experience necessary." Sales-related job ads specified that only a positive attitude and an eagerness to learn were needed.

Getting a job was easy. Keeping it was the problem. Early on, I would realize that I just didn't like the work, or that it was too demanding. After a few weeks, I'd quit.

Knowing I didn't *have* to work made it easy to quit. Of course, if I wanted to be independent, I needed to work. The fact was, though, I didn't need to work to put bread on the table or to make my next rent payment. My parents were always there to pay the bills, so why be miserable at a job I didn't like? My spirit was willing, but my flesh was weak.

I tried waitressing. I hated that line of work.

Initially, quite a few sales jobs held a certain appeal because they promised a high income based on commissions so my earnings were theoretically unlimited, but that was easier said than done. I tried selling everything from luggage to perfumes but found sales to be extremely difficult, especially cold canvassing.

I even tried a sales job at MCI with a friend I knew from Linden Hill. MCI was hiring sweeps of people for telemarketing. We had to call random people and read the same pitch over and over again. I did okay at it, but it soon became too monotonous.

Next, I took a job at Carvel. A regular part of that job was to make hundreds of flying saucer ice cream sandwiches and package them. I gave that job one full week before I was out of there.

It was just too easy to fall back on Dad to pay all the bills. He even invited me to accompany him to the grocery store when he did Mom's weekly shopping. I would meet him there with the car he'd bought me, get my own shopping cart, and he'd pay for whatever I put in it.

It wasn't the guilt of taking their money that bothered me. At that time, I was bitterly convinced they owed me something after all they had put me through, but I knew in my heart of hearts that being connected to them would hinder my growth. How was I ever going to find a job I truly enjoyed and make enough money to support myself?

As much as I wanted to take their money, I intuitively knew that doing so kept me captive to their harmful influence on my life. I knew I had to break away totally. I had no interest in talking to them, but I was forced to be connected to them to the extent that I needed their money, and that didn't always turn out well.

On many an ugly occasion, I would mistakenly mention to them that they were the cause of my problems. I never started out yelling. I just calmly made a simple, matter-of-fact comment. Of course, my parents never received that calmly, and things would quickly escalate. Fueled by their combative fear and self-protective instincts, my statement quickly evolved into their screams of repetitive expletives.

Then, motivated by necessity, I would grovel back to them to apologize. What a way to live!

I wondered about those many years when my parents sat at home to have dinner alone because their children were both institutionalized in mental hospitals. Didn't it ever cross their minds that maybe they might have contributed in some way to their children's' years of hospitalizations? They apparently never considered examining themselves because they had to believe they were perfect. Never would an apology be forthcoming from them.

At one point, under calmer circumstances, I had asked them to pay for my college tuition. Without even considering or discussing it, they said no.

"What about 'ask and you shall receive?'" I asked.

"You haven't been the kind of daughter to us that you should have been. Because of the way you've treated us, you don't deserve for us to pay that kind of money."

Since when does a child have to deserve an education? They certainly had the money.

Even before I asked them to pay for college, I suspected they wouldn't. They had both been denied that opportunity due to the Depression. My dad wasn't even able to finish high school. It wasn't that they didn't want to see their children have the opportunities they never had. They gave us everything we asked for materially, but I think not being able to go to college was still a sore spot for both of them that might not ever fully heal. It would be better not to have any financial connection or obligation to them anyway.

One day, I found a brochure in the mail that offered an associate degree in two years, part-time, at no cost if I qualified for financial aid. I inquired about it at the Westchester Business

Institute and discovered that financial aid would cover everything, including books.

I intentionally chose the night program so I could keep my days open in hopes of eventually finding the right day job. The work required at this business college was easy. I did all my work diligently and earned straight A's.

During the two years of night school, I worked during the day sporadically. On the positive side, I encountered various work environments and different types of people. That provided invaluable experience in helping me determine what I *didn't* want for my career.

I stuck with business school and finished with an associate degree in Business Administration-Management/Marketing, graduating with honors.

While working intermittently and going to school at night, I began what was to become a long pursuit to find answers to the questions that stirred incessantly within me. Being alone in my apartment, I had time to think and seek answers.

Growing up, I had a general belief in God, but He always seemed too distant, and I tended to think He was mad at me. As a child, I sometimes found myself fearing the unknown about death. On a few occasions, the glaring reality that one day I would die caused me long moments of intense fear—not that I thought I was going to die soon, but I knew it would happen eventually, and the thought was petrifying. What would happen when I died, I wondered. Was this life all there was? Would I just cease to exist? I never mentioned these worries to my parents.

Coupled with a basic fear of death was an ever-present yearning to fill what had become an undeniable void in my heart. It was not merely a longing for the love I had never received at home but more of a gaping dissatisfaction with life and a hunger for something to fill me spiritually.

My daily pursuits in life were good, but school and work didn't seem to satisfy me at all. I desperately needed to have hope in something. What could I find that would turn my emptiness into meaning and life's uncertainties into real answers?

My next-door neighbor, Lou, was an ardent Hare Krishna devotee. He was known in the building as "Crazy Lou." Whenever I asked Lou some of life's deep questions, he had an answer for every one. Lou could ramble on indefinitely about things that didn't even make sense to anybody, hence the nickname, but he spouted all sorts of interesting philosophies that seemed to offer some answers to the mysteries of life. He was convinced of his teachings. I was definitely impressed with his conviction.

I hoped he really did have the answers, the real truth. I felt compelled to check it out. In my desperation, I looked into the Hare Krishna religion, wanting those answers he assured me they knew: Why are we here? Is there an afterlife? Is there really a way to eternal bliss like they claimed? I even drove out to Brooklyn to one of their temples and embraced their way of life. For a period of time, I believed their philosophies and totally immersed myself in it all. I never did anything halfway. I had to give this a fair shake.

But this pursuit didn't have a happy ending, only a frightening one. In my zeal I believed, as they taught, that if I sat in their temple and continually repeated a chant of their god while touching a successive bead for each chant, I could reach a state of enlightenment.

Sitting on the floor along with the other people scattered around, also on the floor in different areas inside the temple, I repeated the Hare Krishna chant over and over while touching each bead in my bead bag for each chant. I don't know why I was doing such a crazy thing. I was just searching so desperately that I had to try it out. As I was chanting, an intense terror suddenly swept over me. My heart began to beat frantically. I somehow knew my life was in danger. Not a physical danger, obviously—I was just sitting there—but that sense of doom was clear and dreadful.

As though my life depended on it, I quickly stood up and fled from that place. I had no idea at that time what was going on, but I sped out of there and never looked back. All I knew was that the Hare Krishna thing was definitely not good. Years later, I realized that God had lovingly taken me out of there to protect me from worshiping and giving myself over fully to something evil and being lost forever.

Although that experience proved not to hold the answers I sought, Eastern religions seemed to address those heavy questions about life and still made sense to me. I pursued those ideas with commitment and a renewed sense of hope and passion. I began to study Hinduism, Buddhism, and transcendental meditation.

I really tried to make each new philosophy or religious tenet a full part of my life and integrate it into my thinking. In my enthusiasm, I believed and even preached with conviction whatever it was I was into at the time. After a couple years of giving Eastern religions a thorough try, I was again left with no hope of filling my empty, longing heart.

My pursuits continued. I must have read every popular self-help book in existence, hoping that there was some untapped key to true happiness. Indeed, those books made a lot of lofty claims, all promising paths to true happiness and inner peace, success, and a purposeful life. They all made sense as I read them, and each contained small bits of useless truth, but ultimately, they were filled with what I could only describe as fluff—no real substance.

How could I have read all that stuff and not found any answers? There had to be something real out there.

My search, however, took a brief backseat, as a unique opportunity to be financially free from my parents presented itself. When I saw my chance, I boldly and rapidly moved out of my apartment.

Chapter 8

BREAKING AWAY

IN THE NEWSPAPER'S CLASSIFIED SECTION, I DISCOVered an offer for free room and board in exchange for taking care of horses. No experience was required. This arrangement offered the perfect opportunity to get away from my parents' financial hold on me. If I was courageous enough to just make the break, this was my chance. I was so close to freedom I could taste it.

Up to this point, I'd been living in this apartment for about two years. I went on the interview and, along with a bunch of other young adults, I got the job. Motivated and happy, I quickly put an ad in the paper for my tag sale.

My father warned me not to do it. "Where are you going? What are you going to do? You're making a big mistake."

My mother advised me to give Adam a portion of the money I received from my tag sale, since most of the stuff in the apartment was his. That was something I had already planned on doing.

Surprisingly, hordes of people came. I got rid of everything, even the furniture. I was happy to give Adam what was duly his. As it turned out, he was actually surprised by how much I gave him.

After a week at the horse stables, I was fired for having words with a co-worker. I didn't exactly like the job anyway. It was hard labor, mucking stalls a good part of the day.

No way did I want to go back home.

Andrea, a friend from Linden Hill, and I had maintained phone contact and had also gotten together on a few occasions. She lived in Queens with her mother in a cramped apartment. She also had a six-month-old baby girl and no man in her life. She said my cat, Argentina, and I could stay with her.

Needless to say, living with them was awkward. Her mom did nothing but rant and rave and complain all day. She was confined to bed, seemingly by her own choosing, and drank excessively. This arrangement didn't last long.

With no other options, I called my parents. Against my mother's protests, they took me back home.

Living with my parents felt like being thrown backward in the game of life. Not able to feel any more defeated, I decided to do the sensible yet difficult thing. Although I didn't think of myself as a "live-at-the-Y" kind of person, I put myself on the waiting list to live at the YWCA on North Broadway in White Plains, two towns away from my parent's house. Judgmentally, I believed only low-lifes, old women, and the poor lived at the Y. Moving into the Y seemed like a crutch, like I wasn't really living out on my own.

As the days of living with my parents stretched on, though, the Y looked more and more like paradise. I wanted to get away from them, that focus never changed, but now I only wanted it more. We didn't fight; that was pointless. I simply tolerated them with patient endurance. When I finally got the call to move into the Y, I was actually ecstatic.

Since the rent at the Y was substantially cheaper than an apartment, and utilities, phone, and parking were all included, I could pay for the Y and all of my expenses with the meager SSI check I was getting that my dad had signed me up for while I was living at Linden Hill. Also, at that time, he had put me on Medicaid. Since my various stints in the workforce were so short-lived, I hadn't lost those coverages.

To my utter joy, I was finally financially independent from my parents. Yes, I was reliant upon SSI, but no longer financially dependent on my parents. Another goal achieved! I stopped talking to my parents. It wasn't a conscious choice. It just happened.

Ironically, the Y turned out to be a very enjoyable place to live. A few doors down from me was a girl about my age, Susan. We became close friends and hung out together every day.

Susan had a close friend, Fred, with whom she would get together every week or so. She explained that they were just friends and that she could never like him in any other way. He seemed very interesting—tall, slim, and good looking with blond hair and blue eyes. I found myself wondering if he would like me.

I was happily surprised when Susan thought that Fred and I might be good for each other and arranged a date for us. We hit it off and began seeing each other.

Fred was a very nice person, about my age, but he was a bit shy and somewhat passive. He came from a large family and was still living at home with his parents. Fred was working at an architectural firm as an apprentice and making good money. He was also very talented with drawing and had painted many really good pieces of art. He offered me several of his paintings of my choosing, which he hung up on the walls of my room at the Y.

Living at home with no expenses and having the job he did, he had money and a nice car. We frequently dined out, went to the movies, or anywhere I wanted to go.

I was enjoying quite the life living at the Y. I had a spacious room with a TV, a car, a best friend, and a boyfriend with a nice car and lots of money.

While living at the Y, I decided to take a course to become a Home Health Aide. A lot of young women living there went into that line of work. After a two-week course and receiving a certificate, I wound up taking a couple of one-day jobs (one, an overnight) in the homes of elderly women.

I didn't know the exact job specs of a Home Health Aide, but I quickly realized the clients thought my main purpose for being in their homes was to be their maid. I spent the bulk of my time doing the cleaning that the elderly women were unable or unwilling to do, even though there seemed to be other able-bodied adults in the house.

Then I got the dream job—a part-time, permanent job as a Home Health Aide at a private nursing home in a beautiful section of Larchmont, right near a scenic park overlooking Long Island Sound.

I actually loved the job. I was there from 9:00 a.m. to 1:00 p.m., Monday through Friday. The staff at the nursing home made the beds and took care of the cleaning. My client, Sally, required only companionship and was mentally intact and pleasant. I did nothing but sit there and watch TV with her until lunch time. I ate lunch with this kind, elderly lady at noon every day in their sunlit dining room before I left for the day. The food was actually pretty good, and it was free.

The waiter/attendant, a sort of jack of all trades, Jose, had a thing for me and insisted I order whatever I wanted. Then I would go home to the wonderful Y and go out with Fred after his nine-to-five job.

I stayed at this job a while and became good friends with Jose. He liked his job and was always cheerful and very kind to the elderly occupants. He also worked at the front desk, made repairs, and lived there in an attic apartment.

Sally's daughter was very happy with me. "We finally picked a winner," she exclaimed. Not exactly the nurturing type back then, I was rather surprised by that. Who might they have had before me? I wondered.

The daughter actually offered me a beach pass at a place nearby to use over the upcoming summer. I hadn't planned on working over the summer, however. I had every intention of enjoying my summer with Fred and Susan and not being strapped down to a job that would eat away the first half of my day. When summer came, I quit.

That decision probably seemed unwise, but I wound up having a great summer with Fred and Susan, and I wanted to go back to college that fall anyway. Fred was planning on going to SUNY (State University of New York) Purchase in the fall, majoring in art and living on campus.

As the fall neared, I decided to enroll at the same school that semester with Fred. Although I had an associate degree from a business school, that didn't seem like a real college. I had only gotten that degree out of convenience. Business was interesting, but I didn't want to make a career out of it. Back then, I thought it represented what my dad stood for—being an entrepreneur, pushing a product on people that they could probably do without, and charging as much as he could get away with in order to make the best possible profit. I wanted a different major and a "real" college experience.

At SUNY Purchase, I chose to major in Environmental Science, my heart's passion at that time. I hoped this pursuit would be the thing to fulfill me.

Going to a state school was relatively inexpensive. I was able to get partial financial aid. In addition, without having applied, I received a partial tuition scholarship from a women's organization I'd never heard of based on the straight A's I'd received from the Westchester Business Institute.

At that business school was the first time I'd applied myself in school, and I received good grades and a partial scholarship for my efforts. Monetarily, I had enough to register full-time and live on campus for the year.

One evening before our summer had ended, as Fred and I were taking a walk, I began to wonder if it was a good idea for us to break up so we could embark on our college experience unattached and open to any new relationship or experience that might present itself. Whether or not that was my independent nature kicking in, it seemed like a practical thing to do, and I verbalized it.

Fred thought it was a bad idea, and we argued a little. Unpredictably, he began to cry and beg me not to break up with him. I was shocked. Caught off guard and turned off by his desperation, I immediately made my decision. "I'm sorry. It's over."

The saying, "Be careful what you wish for; you just may get it," aptly described my so-called real college experience. I spent most of my time in my dorm room fantasizing.

My roommate and I actually got along pretty well. Helena was Spanish, very pretty, and intelligent. She had graduated valedictorian from her high school in Florida and wanted to follow in her aunt's footsteps as a filmmaker.

As far as I could see, my roommate's MO seemed to be to acquire friends for the sole purpose of what they could do for her filmmaking career, and by necessity, anything they could do for her immediate needs for money, food, or transportation. That was the key to why we got along so well. I had a car and money.

Without my car, she was stuck on campus eating at the cafeteria or other campus food vendors. Without her friendship, I'd never have gotten out socially. Under the circumstances, it was good for me to spend time with her and her friends, who were nice, incredibly funny, crazy, and very appreciative toward me for my car.

After I'd fantasized for several hours, Helena would show up and ask if I wanted to go out to eat with her and the two male filmmaker friends she hung out with exclusively.

I didn't feel used because our friendship was definitely reciprocal. I spent a few weekends with her at her apartment in Manhattan, which she shared with a friend. Her aunt, who lived nearby, paid her share of the rent. We also went to Florida together over spring break and stayed with her family. That time was fun.

The courses at college were actually very difficult. I had to take chemistry, biology, and labs, which were required for an environmental science major.

The atmosphere was overwhelmingly stressful. I was fearful most of the time when immersed in a social situation, which was whenever I was out of my dorm room.

Because I was a procrastinator, the constant pressure of having to get my work done hung over me. Too out-of-it from fantasizing, I kept hoping I'd have a clearer mind later. Then, at the last minute, I'd have no choice but to do the work.

A continuous party went on in one of the rooms of our dorm. People escaped the pressures of college life by anesthetizing themselves with booze and drugs. I kept to myself and hid out in my room fantasizing. With Helena out every weekend at her apartment in the city, I was free to fantasize nonstop.

So entrenched was I in surviving this morbid college experience, the thought of my parents never entered my mind. Between living at the Y and my time at school, almost two years had passed without calling them. That was fine with me, but apparently that large gap in time got under my father's skin. They'd had no idea about my plans to leave the Y and live at a nearby college. Not knowing where I was caused my dad the sudden and urgent need to locate me. He must have been worried and needed to know I was okay.

One day, I got a call from him on a phone in one of the dorm rooms. We didn't have cell phones back then. I could just imagine how he must have badgered everyone who worked at the Y in order to learn of my whereabouts. Then, he probably called the administration office at SUNY Purchase in the same manner he always did things—yelling and demanding information.

Someone handed me a phone, saying I had a call. "I don't even know where you are?" he began abruptly. "Where have you been all this time?"

I felt intruded upon, like he was an investigator demanding this information as his civic right, not as a concerned father. Not in the mood for this. I told him, "I'm at school, living on campus."

After I gave him the required information, I said nothing more. Seemingly embarrassed and trying to justifying his tone, he said, "Okay, I just wanted to know where you were, if you had disappeared, what had happened to you."

His pride seemed to have been wounded. Never would he admit to himself that his motives for calling me were self-serving, that he was worried more about looking stupid for not being privy to my whereabouts than caring about my well-being. Whether that assessment was accurate or not, I just didn't feel love from him or that he was calling me out of genuine fatherly concern.

"Okay, bye." I said.

I quickly forgot about that strange phone call and moved on. I had a life of my own to live, albeit a dark and miserable one.

I fantasized practically every waking moment, just barely making it to class. Not until the deadline became imminent did I rush to complete my assignments. I began to chain-smoke, especially when I was working on a paper. I was sick with a cold every month. My dream of a real college experience didn't at all match the constant fear and dismal existence of that life—another pursuit that wasn't living up to expectations, but I somehow wasn't ready to give up.

As the school year finally came to an end, I was registered for full-time classes and all set to return the following fall and to live on campus again, but I hadn't planned for the summer in between. Getting through the school year took all of my effort just to survive. As summer break finally arrived, so did my panic about where to stay.

Chapter 9

Looking for Love in All the Wrong Places

I DECIDED THE MOST LOGICAL THING TO DO WAS TO become a summer camp counselor at a sleep-away camp, where I would get paid and also have a place to live.

While looking for a camp counselor position, I stayed with Jose, the guy who worked at the nursing home and had his own attic apartment there. He was happy to have me. Nothing was going on beyond friendship, even though he wanted more.

Probably since I had waited until the last minute, I couldn't find any jobs at a sleep-away camp, only day camps, despite my diligent search. Finally, I found what I assumed was a job at a sleep-away camp by the way the ad was worded, but it hadn't specified either way. When I went on the interview, I was disappointed to discover that it was, in fact, a day camp.

Nevertheless, the owner told me about a family with two boys who attended his camp every summer. The mother was looking for a "mother's helper" who would live with them just over the summer in exchange for taking care of the kids and light housekeeping. I would be expected to drive the kids to and from day camp as well as, of course, work at the camp during the day.

That sounded perfect. After an interview with the mother, Francesca, I was hired and began to work both as a mother's helper and a camp counselor.

I enjoyed my summer living with this well-off family in their nice house. Although I was the nanny, they accepted me as part of their family. I pretty much did everything with them, including waterskiing on their boat on weekends. Many nights, after the boys went to bed, I spent time talking with Francesca and her husband, Edward. Although I didn't get paid, Francesca generously supplied the various things I needed.

During my stay with this family, my parents retired, sold the printing business and the house, and moved to Florida. My brother decided to stay in New York. He got an apartment and continued to work at our dad's old printing shop under the new owner. Not surprisingly, that didn't last long.

Being a type-A workaholic, Dad was not content to enjoy his retirement. He offered to help Adam build up his own printing business in Florida. Adam would get a house near my parents, and Dad would help him with his business until he was able to run it on his own. Not a bad arrangement. Of course, Adam said yes to that.

As the summer waned and my camp counselor job ended, it was time to leave this family's home and go back to school. I had definitely enjoyed the summer taking care of the boys, and the feeling was mutual. The idea of continuing to live with them and commuting to SUNY Purchase had come up. The boys wanted me to stay, and I thought it would be a good idea, so the parents and I decided I would stay on.

Being wanted by them made me feel loved and accepted. I'd always wanted to be part of a loving family. Maybe this was the family I'd always dreamed of. After all those years of fantasizing about having different parents, here it seemed to be a reality—a dream come true.

In the mornings after working to get the boys off to school, I commuted to my classes. When they came home, I took care of them and did some of the housecleaning.

Over a short period of time, I found myself less interested in my classes and more concerned about the demands of this family. As the importance of school diminished, I dropped courses one by one since they seemed to conflict with my family life. Francesca managed to convince me that Environmental Science wasn't a good major for me and was a waste of time. She was right. I really wasn't interested in that major. By the middle of the semester, I quit college altogether.

There I was, twenty-four and a full-time nanny. I began to confide in Francesca about my fantasy life. Not about getting love from different parents—that would have been too awkward—but just the fact that it existed, the hours I spent doing it, and how guilty I felt afterward.

Although my dream life had been a means of survival at one time, I knew it was wrong to continue at this point. It used up much of my energy and left me tired, guilt-ridden, and out of sorts. Fortunately, I was kept so busy with household chores and the demands of childcare that I scarcely had time to fantasize during the day. But at night I would indulge, even to the point of losing sleep.

Although being busy definitely cut down on it, it was still an addiction. I couldn't seem to go more than a day without it, despite my continued attempts to stop. At night, when my work was done, I would go for a long drive, music playing, and with free abandon, let my heart soar, spending several blissful hours dreaming away.

Afterward, of course, I felt like an alcoholic who'd just binged—guilt-ridden and disoriented. My frame of mind was noticeable to Francesca, who would tell me that I had a "shit-eating grin" on my face and would ask me condescendingly if I'd been bad.

It didn't take long for the normalcy of our relationship to decline. Of course, I was coming from a place of need. Although my outward façade convincingly portrayed otherwise, I was vastly lacking in enough self-esteem to protect myself from anyone wanting to take advantage of me.

Since I was around during the day and Francesca didn't work, we had a lot of time to talk while the kids were at school and her husband was at work. I told her about my suicide attempts and subsequent hospitalizations and about my early family life.

My connection with the outside world had ceased. I'd cut ties with my former friends and with school. Sadly, Francesca was the only relationship I had and the only connection I seemed to want.

Here was a family who accepted me even after they knew everything about me. They entrusted me with their kids, their cars, and their money. This seemed to be what I'd always dreamed of. For once, I felt needed, a part of something real, not a fantasy. Unlike my parents, they appreciated me. They praised my efforts and gave me the approval I'd always longed for.

It was clear what I was getting out of this whole thing, pitiful as it was. But besides all the work I did for them, what were Francesca and her husband getting out of this unusual arrangement?

I wasn't supposed to work there during the days, just nights and weekends to cover my room and board. I wasn't, after all, getting paid a dime. Since I wasn't working at a camp or taking college courses, I filled my days trying to win her approval while also keeping busy. I ran her errands, did her grocery shopping, and various other tasks she could think of.

It seemed Francesca played on my need for approval. I was eager to impress her, and she seemed to feel justified in giving me more things to do because she knew that with any free time on my hands, I would only use it to indulge my bad habit. And we all knew *that* was not good for me. Oddly, the word *fantasize* became a household word.

She tried to solve my problems, but in the process, all she could really do was point out my deficiencies. I sensed she had a tendency to compare herself to me, and then gloat about her own superiority.

In this relationship, she became the mother. She seemed to need that. Unfortunately, I needed and wanted motherly approval more than anything in the world, but to her that was a sign of weakness. I gradually began to realize that this wasn't the healthy relationship I'd initially thought.

In fact, on a few occasions, I came in contact with a particular couple, Pam and Carl, at some of the boys' outside activities. Francesca and Pam had maintained a friendly rapport over the years. Their boys had played together at one point. Pam was divorced and seeing Carl, who was a lot older than she.

Pam and Carl seemed to have noticed that something wasn't right about how Francesca treated me and told me kindly that they believed I was in a bad situation and being taken advantage of.

The boys' tutor was strikingly more blatant in his assessment of my role in that household. "How does it feel to be a slave?" he once asked me when I began to clip one of the boys' toenails upon his request.

When I told my former college roommate, Helena, that I'd quit college to work as a full-time nanny, not surprisingly, she exclaimed, "What! Are you crazy?"

I got to know Pam and Carl a little here and there. Sympathetic toward my situation, they suggested I get out of that arrangement. Carl even told me that since all of his kids had grown up and moved out, and he was living alone, I was welcome to stay at his house. He was hardly ever there, he explained, and it was a waste to have all those empty rooms not being used. He knew I didn't have a job, so he mentioned that I could do some light cleaning in exchange.

I didn't act on his offer immediately. But things were getting progressively worse living with this family. I hadn't seen clearly how insidiously over time my situation had evolved to the point of abuse. Francesca yelled at me regularly, verbally demeaned me, threatened to throw me out, and on one occasion, actually hit me.

One day, we were having another heated argument, and knowing what would upset her, I restated something that her cleaning lady had once told me about her. As expected, incensed by what I'd repeated, she hauled off and punched me in the head. Feeling that she'd behaved like a criminal and that I deserved better, I finally found the strength to leave that house.

Disappointed that yet another pursuit of happiness had gone bad, I hurriedly packed my things and drove straight over to Carl's house.

True to his word, Carl gladly offered me my choice of any of the four empty, sun-filled bedrooms in his house. I picked one, thanked him profusely, and began to settle in. I wondered momentarily about his children. Based on how nice a person he was, I imagined they were all off to bright careers and families of their own.

I also wondered at the inappropriateness of this living situation. There I was, young, slim, and pretty, living in this guy's house, while he was old enough to be my grandfather. Clearly, he wasn't interested in me, and that was the last thing on my mind.

The situation was pretty amazing. It seemed too good to be true. He worked all week and spent his evenings and weekends at his girlfriend, Pam's, house. I rarely saw him. It was like having my own house, everything included, and no expenses.

He even gave me a twenty here and there when we rarely crossed paths, like the proverbial two ships passing in the night. Truth be told, I never did any cleaning, and he never noticed or cared. I was accountable to absolutely no one. Talk about going from one extreme to the other! Living in Carl's house was in stark contrast to my previous arrangement, but it turned out to be a mixed blessing.

In my previous environment, I had structure to each day as the routines of a family life required. Like a concerned mother, Francesca was interested in my whereabouts and my activities every second of the day. That was one of the reasons I had initially liked it there. No one had ever taken that kind of interest in me.

Due to all the structure and busyness, I was only able to manage about three to four hours of fantasizing a day. At this new home, I had time on my side and absolutely no demands from anyone. Unfortunately, those were the ingredients for disaster.

With nothing to do twenty-four/seven, fantasizing became a way of life. I didn't want to do it. I knew it was wrong. I would promise myself "just five minutes." It was always "just five minutes." How stupid that was. Six hours later, I was still dreaming away.

I'd get out of bed to get some food and then drive around with the music on and fantasize some more. It always made my heart race and my adrenaline flow. Just as others can drive and talk, I was able to simultaneously drive and fantasize. Strangely, I was more capable of avoiding a car accident because I was so pumped up than if I wasn't fantasizing. And I could put it on hold until I got on the highway or whenever I needed to.

In this empty house, all alone, just fantasizing for hours upon hours, day after day and into the night, I had to wonder if maybe I wasn't better off at that family's house with all the structure, routines, chores, and kids to play with. Or maybe, when comparing the two, it was just a matter of which one was the least detrimental.

Obviously, being with that abusive woman was dead wrong for me. Everything about that place was oppressive. I had no autonomy whatsoever. But being alone, having free room and board, and not having to work was disastrous.

For a couple of months, I did nothing but eat, sleep, and fantasize—in bed, in the car, for hours. I would go for eleven-hour marathons. It was way out of control.

Each day, I knew I was playing with fire. What if I went into a fantasy and enjoyed it so much I never came out? What if I had a heart attack? I couldn't go on like this. It was scary. I was totally non-functional. That was my main concern. I was actually not functioning. I had to do something that could help me overcome this addiction. I had to get control of this and stop it completely.

I knew it was wrong because it was an escape, and it left me depleted of energy. My imagination could never give me the love and approval I'd never received. I was no longer a child. I had to give up this dependency.

I'd always assumed I had the power to stop. It never occurred to me that I couldn't stop on my own. After so many years, especially as a child, this means of escape had been integrated into every fiber of my being. It was as much a physical way of life as it was an emotional one.

Unfortunately, I still hadn't realized yet that I couldn't control it on my own, but I did know that I needed to figure out how to stop it in a more radical, proactive way than to *just keep trying*. That wasn't working.

My immediate mission became to figure out a way to permanently stop this addiction so I could be healthy and functional. I had to be able to function. I couldn't just let this problem, by now like a disease, continue to ruin my life and render me a helpless vegetable lying in bed all day. Thank God, I got out of Francesca's house, or I might not have realized how bad this addiction could get.

I didn't know what to do, though. How could I get help? I understood by the nature of this problem that it was addictive. When I tried to limit it to only five minutes, I couldn't stop. I was just like an alcoholic who says, "Just one drink," and then finds herself in a drunken stupor. I had to stop cold turkey.

But how many people have this particular addiction? There's Alcoholics Anonymous, Narcotics Anonymous, and so on, but I'd never heard of Fantasizers Anonymous. I needed to do something, so I joined Alcoholics Anonymous.

It really wasn't a joke to me. I was at rock bottom, and I believed if I embraced "the program" that it could truly work for me. It worked for so many other people. I just needed to substitute in my mind (and keep secret from everyone else) the words *fantasy* or *fantasizing* with the words *alcohol* or *drinking*.

It had to work. I had an addiction. The same principles applied for all the other addictions, and I desperately wanted to stop my dependence. It shouldn't matter *what* my compulsion was. The program should work for all addictions, and I was going to make this work.

This may seem like an oversimplification, but I didn't know what else to do. I was definitely grasping at straws. In desperation, I called the AA number, and they were more than happy to help me with my so-called alcohol addiction. I actually began to feel hopeful.

They gave me a list of all the meetings that were going on in my area, and I attended quite a few of them. It wasn't like I had a busy schedule. I was also given a sponsor who drove me to some of the meetings.

Although I had once, years ago, tried several drinks on one occasion to see what it was like to get drunk, I didn't like it. It tasted disgusting and made me sleepy. I concluded there was absolutely no fun in that and never drank again. Still, it was easy to identify with the other people there because they all had an addiction just like I did. They weren't crazy or mentally ill, just addicted to alcohol. It's a noble thing to try to get help for that.

In the midst of what felt like a dark, lonely road, I attended those meetings with eager anticipation and met with my sponsor. I never told anyone the real reason I was there. At times, I felt fleeting glimmers of hope, but I always wound up going back to fantasizing.

So sure that this would help, I stuck with AA for two to three months. Of course, it didn't. I still fantasized excessively. With nowhere else to turn, I did the unthinkable.

Chapter 10

THE UNTHINKABLE

UTTERLY DEFEATED, WITH NOWHERE ELSE TO TURN, I did what to me was categorically unthinkable. I went to see a psychotherapist. I had thought I was done with that part of my life. I wasn't mentally ill. I just had an inability to stop fantasizing. Okay, maybe that was a little abnormal.

My fantasy life was a means of survival a long time ago, but now it had become a debilitating stumbling block to accomplishing my goals. What was once such a helpful pastime in my early life had taken on a life of its own, an addiction run amok. I had to throw off this crippling burden. Now, I had to go back to the mental health scene again. That annoyed me.

Having Medicaid, I went to a mental health clinic nearby to see a therapist. As it turned out, he was a very nice, down-to-earth guy. I explained to him that I needed to be able to stop the fantasizing and that I also had self-esteem and trust issues.

He seemed to understand exactly what I was going through. To my surprise, he said he had good news for me. In the midst of my miserable addictive plague, a ray of hope suddenly shone through.

He explained that there was a new unit at New York Hospital that dealt with people with my type of issues. They had cutting edge approaches in group and individual therapy.

Was he saying to go back into a mental hospital? Why would that be good news? To me it sounded purely insane, no pun intended.

Yet, he somehow stirred my interest by explaining that it was a unique opportunity, and he was sure it would help me stop fantasizing for good. I had to consider what he was promising, the thing I so desperately wanted—to actually be able to stop this addiction. Free from that, I could live a successful life.

At this point, what else could I do? Continue to see him one hour a week and fantasize the other endless hours? I couldn't live like that. I had reached rock bottom, and I was desperate.

I remembered that, unlike RCPC, which was a state run, hellish place to be, New York Hospital was a very nice private facility. At age fourteen, I had been there for a ninety-day observation period following my suicide attempt. During those early years of treatment, if you could call it that, I was unwilling and truly unable to help myself. I was just a child, programmed to be what I was, and unable to defy my parents and change myself. I had also been hospitalized entirely against my will.

Now, I was an adult and would be there by my own choice. I had a chance to fix this. What other option did I have? Maybe this really was my chance to realize my long-desired goal to be completely free from my past and its destructive effects.

Additionally, my therapist made it sound new and exciting, not like a traditional hospital. That this unit was for young adults with problems just like mine intrigued me. I honestly didn't realize other people had problems just like mine.

What made me suitable for this unique unit was, he told me, that I had Obsessive Compulsive Disorder (OCD) and that everyone on that unit had Borderline Personality Disorder. Was that something real, or did they just have to put a name on everything, I wondered.

In today's fast-paced world, it seems that everyone has OCD, and it can almost be a good thing. These days, it's even fashionable to be OCD, and some professions even boast about having it. But back then, it was virtually unheard of.

Obviously, I had OCD. What had I been doing for the last twenty some odd years but dreaming repetitively about the same thing. In my childhood anguish, I learned the desperate act of obsessing on what I needed.

Having Borderline Personality Disorder was another thing. I learned that that handle described a certain group of people that weren't really mentally ill (psychotic) but were never loved, were repeatedly rejected, and became emotionally needy and confused as to how to meet those needs in healthy ways—neurotic, not psychotic, hence borderline. That could describe more than half the population, to varying degrees.

Because these individuals were never loved, they had a difficult time loving themselves. Instead of meeting their healthy, normal needs for love and approval in beneficial ways, they tended to use negative, harmful ways, such as unhealthy relationships, bad choices, addictions, and hurting themselves. I could relate to all of that.

I agreed to take action and finally get to the bottom of my problems and get rid of the fantasizing. Despite all my prior affirmations that I would never again be associated with the mental health field and all its stigmas, now I wanted to be well so badly, I was willing to put myself into a mental hospital.

There was a waiting list, however. The other catch was that I had to go for an interview to see if I was appropriate for this unique opportunity.

The director of the program, an elderly lady, interviewed me. Small in stature, she chose her words exceedingly carefully as she spoke with an air of dignity. At the conclusion of the interview, she told me she saw potential in me and that I seemed to be motivated toward my treatment.

Only days after the interview, I got a call saying I was accepted. I was very glad. Oddly, I felt wanted. Finally, I might actually get the help I needed. I was put on the waiting list and told I would get a call when there was an opening, i.e., a bed available. It was just a matter of waiting.

Next, I did the unthinkable *again*. I reasoned that rather than wait around dreaming all day long in that empty house, it made sense to go back to Francesca's. Soon I'd be leaving anyway. Why not enjoy the ski trips, the summer boating, the clothes, the attention, the structure, and the good food? One last fling, so to speak.

I called and told her everything that was going on. As it turned out, despite the ever-present grapevine, she didn't know I had been staying at Carl's house. In fact, since I had left on such bad terms, and they had no idea what I might do, they had changed the code on their security system.

Despite our last episode, I apparently hadn't completely burned my bridges. Francesca wanted me back. She was also happy I was going to get the help I needed and understood that I was only staying until my name came up on the waiting list.

I'll never forget what my therapist said when I told him I was going back to her house. In shocked disbelief he asked, "Are you a glutton for punishment? She hits you in the head, and you go back for more?"

And he was being literal. It sounded like a stupid decision when he put it that way. And it turned out to be a stupid decision. A person who loved herself would never willingly go back into such a degrading situation. Foolishly, though, I believed it was better to be *there* functioning again than waiting around at Carl's house fantasizing endlessly.

My choice was a matter of the lesser of two bondages—the bondage to the addiction or to that of being subjected to my position in that household. My purpose, in every sense of the word, was to be their slave. I didn't get paid. I did all the chores and anything else that was asked of me, and Francesca knew where I was at all times. That basically defines the term "slave," except that I was there by choice.

I can't fault them entirely. They obviously trusted me and, in their own way, cared about me. They shared their entire lives with me. Despite the strange nature of our relationship, in retrospect, there were some good times and fond memories.

It just seemed to make sense to go back there, where I would have structure and human interaction, rather than lie in bed all day and night fantasizing. Being there the second time, though, it became clear to me that I deserved so much more out of life.

As the days trudged along, I really began to abhor the demeaning aspects of this arrangement. I couldn't wait to get out of this house and be free from washing their dishes, doing their laundry, and vacuuming their cars. I couldn't wait for the call to get me out of that house. You would think I was on a waiting list for a ball. But unlike Cinderella, I wasn't exactly going to ride in a coach and meet a prince.

As I folded their laundry, I vowed to myself that I would never fold a man's underwear again unless it was my own husband's in my own house. And, incidentally, that's a vow I kept.

The call finally came. I had been waiting for about two months, which felt like two years. By this time, I was very excited about heading into this new venture. I wanted a cure for my addiction, and that was the only reason I wanted to do this.

All the other patients on this unit were very intelligent and articulate. I felt intimidated. During my childhood, I'd only learned how to withdraw and shut everyone out. I'd become an introvert. In my understanding of life, people were only out to hurt me. As a result, I hadn't developed the set of social skills these young adults all possessed. Although to some extent I knew I was intelligent, I believed other people thought I was stupid. Due to my lack of social skills and self-esteem, I came across that way.

Although the patients on this unit, who were all about my age, in our twenties, were socially more mature and more refined in the art of communication than I, they clearly came from a place of severe difficulty. Something had happened to them, and they needed to talk about it. They too required intervention at this time in their lives.

The mode of therapy involved excessive confrontation from your peers, as well as from the mental health team, who incited the battle. During the daily group sessions, one person was the "scapegoat," and everyone else made negative observations about that person's behavior or character flaws that needed to be changed. The idea was to help the person get out of denial and see the reality of their inappropriate behaviors or poor decisions.

Several times throughout my stay, the unit doctor offered me medication, but I turned it down. The physically weakening I'd experienced with the array of medications I'd been on as a teenager at RCPC didn't make me eager to try that option again. As soon as I could, I'd gotten off all medications and intended never to consider that idea again. Since I was there voluntarily, they couldn't force me.

Up to this point, I didn't fully grasp that I couldn't stop fantasizing on my own. I always assumed I was capable of stopping if I tried hard enough. As it turned out, getting into this hospital on this particular unit was actually a medical necessity because I couldn't stop fantasizing on my own. But God was behind the scenes getting me the help I needed when I was fully ready.

Further along in my stay, I was once again offered medication, and by some miracle, I agreed. It must have been a move of God in my heart because I just thought, why not*?* They explained to me that this medication was something entirely new and different than what I had taken years ago, and it had helped many people with the same sort of OCD that I had.

The drug I started on was, at that time, considered to be a new miracle drug, Prozac. Of course, today it's very popular, but back then it was the new wonder drug out on the market. By God's grace, it turned out to be a miracle for me!

Survival modes we develop in our early years can create serious problems for us later on. These need to be fixed, sometimes by medication. My fantasizing, which had started out as a means of survival in a very dark and evil home, had grown into an addiction that was out of control. Back then, I had no choice but to obsess the way I did.

After being on Prozac for a short period of time, I finally understood that the reason I'd never stopped fantasizing, despite all my efforts, was because I couldn't. Prozac turned out to be God's instrument of healing. Shortly after I began taking it, I no longer had a desire to fantasize. I even tried to do it out of curiosity but found I was unable to get it going. This medication had made me nonobsessive, and I was no longer *able* to fantasize. That was a miracle!

I had more energy, and I felt a million times happier. My life at New York Hospital began to move in a positive direction. I was seeing a really nice therapist, who was young, very dedicated, and whom I began to connect with and trust. She was very enthusiastic about my progress and communicated that to me and the staff. I was finally able to stop the addictive behavior, have the energy and focus I needed, and feel extremely happy.

Based on our progress, patients were assigned levels of status on this unit, and my level enabled me to get a volunteer job at the hospital library. I was astounded that I was able to concentrate energetically on tedious clerical work and not tire out. I'd never been able to focus like that before.

Things were going great for the next two months or so—until the team of interns that were on rotation in our unit had to move on. The entire team, including my therapist, was leaving. In addition, the director, who ran the morning community meetings and was an important presence there, was also leaving. He wasn't doing an internship but was switching positions with a doctor from another unit, who had an interest in the treatment of borderline personality patients.

That meant the continuity of treatment would be disrupted. Everyone was going to have to adjust to the change. Because I didn't get emotionally attached to people, I didn't care about the change. In my mind, change was a good thing because I've always believed things could only get better. My therapist, very nostalgic and kind in her goodbye, gave me a picture of herself to help me remember her and our time together.

In came all the new faces. I was given another young therapist, and I was eager to continue doing well. Unfortunately, she seemed indifferent and even a bit flippant. Still, I trusted we could hit it off well. I knew things took time. Observing her in the front office one day, however, I saw what she was all about.

She was young, pretty, and still in school. Seeming to enjoy her new intern status at this prestigious hospital, she had a boastful air that said, "I have arrived." Sadly, she was too full of herself to care about anyone else. Since she was like that with everyone, I didn't take it personally.

Our new director also seemed to be a negative addition to the unit. He was a people pleaser and tended to play favorites with certain patients. Unfortunately, I wasn't one of them. Yet, I was content to continue to do well, even though my new therapist seemed to be more interested in casting judgment than wanting to help me.

But one day, a bizarre incident occurred on the unit that snowballed into disaster. While I was playing ping pong with someone in the hallway one afternoon, another patient, a big guy, lurked in the doorway of his room nearby. While we played our game, he peered strangely at me. I quickly realized he seemed to harbor a sizeable amount of anger toward me.

I didn't actually know why he was mad at me, and I didn't care, but I think it was because of the way I had treated a particular woman in one of our community meetings that morning. Despite being extremely timid and soft-spoken, she had voiced her opinion about something, and I'd disagreed. This guy had spoken up in her defense, probably believing I was unjustly mean to a passive person. Or maybe he liked her.

He was well over six feet tall and known to be volatile. Suddenly, without provocation, he came out of his room and started yelling at me at the top of his lungs.

Although it was a scary situation, I decided not to walk away. He was in the wrong, and I wasn't backing down even though he could have potentially hurt me at any moment. I just stood there and held my ground, as he continued to scream.

Of course, staff members arrived on the scene moments later and told us both to go to our rooms. Their belittling response to this incident disappointed and angered me, since I wasn't the one acting like a child, nor was I the guilty party. Although it might have been for safety reasons, they should have restrained him, and then proceeded to get my side of the story. Summarily, they assumed that I had provoked the guy.

Alone in my room, infuriated at the unfairness, I continued to wait. Not a single staff member came in to ask me if I was okay or to even ask for the details of what had happened.

I felt as if they blamed me and that I was being punished for instigating his episode, even though he had come out of his room perhaps motivated by something that had happened hours before. My anger continued to boil at the unwarranted way I was treated. In my usual way of handling things, I impulsively decided to get out of there.

There was simply no way I could continue to stay in that room or even on that unit. I'd been abused and treated unfairly all my life, especially by an older brother, and nothing was ever done about it. But here? In a hospital? That was too much.

The only real skill I had for resolving conflicts was to run away, quit, move, or fantasize, and I couldn't figure out anything different this time. I had never learned to communicate effectively when problems arose. Running away was the only way I knew how to express to the staff how angry I felt, so I decided to go. I realized that running was a drastic measure, but I wanted to send a clear message that I was upset by the completely undeserved and demeaning manner in which they had treated me.

The idea of communicating verbally to them never entered my mind, especially since everyone was new and no one seemed to be on my side. Who would listen to me or defend me or even believe me? Many years later, though, I would meet Someone who would listen to me, believe in me, fully know and love me, and who would even fight all of my battles for me.

I had run away from this hospital before when things got rough, but I never really got very far because I was either stopped immediately or found quickly and brought back. This time, I was determined not to get caught.

I planned everything this time. Knowing it wasn't easy not to be found within an hour, I waited until dark and wore black. I went out into the hallway and waited close to the door that led out of the unit. Crouching down next to one of the large, comfy chairs, obscured from view, I waited for the next person to enter the unit.

As I waited, I knew I was definitely playing with fire. All of my common sense told me not to go. I knew there would be consequences for this action and that I shouldn't do it. I was taking a big chance. I could jeopardize my stay and ruin my chance at wellness and success.

I had run about five times prior and had been told that if it happened again, I could possibly be kicked out. No way could I afford being kicked out. This was definitely an important juncture in my life. This was my final chance to become well. I couldn't fail at my stay here. I risked everything if I followed through with running away.

But I couldn't stay. My feelings of anger and betrayal were too intense, and they weren't being resolved. Tragically, I was willing to risk throwing away my seemingly last chance at becoming well and having success in life.

Interestingly, as I sat there waiting for the next person to come in that door so I could get out, a song popular at that time played in my head. The lyrics went something like, "Send me an angel, *oo- oo- oo*.... right now."

That song in my head turned into a prayer in my heart to God. Right there in the hallway, I prayed that He would send *me* an angel, half believing, half not taking the idea seriously. Nonetheless, that night He did.

In the pit of my despair, at my lowest moment, He helped me. He didn't send an *actual* angel, though He might as well have. He sent a friend to help me, one who did so with complete unselfishness—a true man of God.

The door to the unit opened and in walked one of the social workers. I casually walked toward the door, smiled, and said, "G.O. status" (grounds only). She smiled pleasantly as she let me out.

I was going to be smart this time. From experience, I knew about the high beam lights they utilized to search out escapees. I found the side of a brick building with lots of shrubbery in front of it. I stationed myself behind some thick bushes and waited motionlessly, blending in perfectly with my dark clothes. This was probably the last place they'd think to look.

As expected, I saw those big lights flashing around as hospital security followed protocol. Finally, less than an hour later, the lights stopped. I guess they deduced that if they didn't find anyone on the grounds within thirty minutes, that person was gone.

I had done it. With infuriated determination, I'd waited them out. Quickly, I ventured out. Not trusting the main driveway, I went into the woods and made my way down the hill toward town. At one point, I even had to jump a fence and managed to cut my hand. To this day, I still have the scar, a reminder of how utterly lost and helpless I'd been and how God lovingly helped me.

During each of the previous times I'd run away, the thought of going back to Francesca's house had been remote. As tempting as it was, I knew it was the wrong thing to do.

Interestingly, but not surprisingly, after my social worker met Francesca when I was first admitted, she told me it wouldn't be good for my treatment to continue to have contact with her. They could see that our relationship was emotionally unhealthy. Apparently, she was considered a bad influence and "off limits." Further, my social worker wanted me to be the one to tell Francesca this in our next and final meeting with her, which I did.

This time, my destination was Francesca's house. Feeling betrayed by the new crew at the hospital, I felt more of an allegiance to her. From the hospital, her house was about a forty-minute drive away. I was able to hitch a couple of rides to a nearby town. Then, as I continued to hitch while walking to her house, a man pulled over and offered me a ride.

We exchanged a little small talk. He lived not far from Francesca's house, and kindly, he drove me all the way there. His name was Bill. As I thanked him and said goodbye, he handed me a piece of paper with his name and phone number and told me to call him if I needed someone to talk to.

At the time, I thought nothing of it. But meeting Bill was no coincidence. I had asked God for an angel, but He sent me something better—a Christian friend who would always be there to help whenever I needed someone and would labor in prayer for me. And he asked nothing in return.

Unmistakably, God was reaching out to me, but I wasn't willing. In fact, I continued in my ignorance to reject Him for many years to follow.

It was about eight o'clock in the evening when I arrived at Francesca's. It was a happy reunion of sorts. We went to the mall, where we ate dinner and she bought me a blouse. We talked a lot, caught up on many things. Eventually, very late, she drove me back to the hospital.

Now that I had returned, I had to face the consequences. I was okay with that. I felt I'd had no choice but to run. What followed, however, was almost impossible to believe because it was so callous, but I remember it to the last detail.

Chapter 11

The Ultimate Rejection

BECAUSE I HAD RUN AWAY FIVE TIMES BEFORE, THE hospital needed to set an example for the other patients. Understandably, it upset the staff and especially the patients that I had taken advantage of the system and had broken that particular rule repeatedly. Up to this point, I had gotten away with it, but they had to set a precedent or everyone would think it was okay to run away.

The decision was made that I had to leave the hospital within two weeks. I could come and go as I pleased during this time only for the purpose of obtaining living arrangements. If I hadn't found a place to live when the two weeks were up, it didn't matter. I would be escorted out of the building.

What swayed their decision most, because it was particularly unsettling, they said, was that I had gone back to Francesca's house.

The fact that I was receiving treatment for not knowing how to effectively communicate my anger and my only learned skill for conflict resolution was to run away didn't seem to have any bearing in their decision-making. My reason for being there had everything to do with my escaping painful situations in non-productive ways. Why kick me out for displaying the very symptoms of the problem I was there for?

Naturally, at the time, I couldn't articulate any of that. It probably wouldn't have made a difference anyway. The unfairness of the incident that spurred this whole situation was never addressed either. I felt like a failure again. I was being kicked out of a mental hospital. Who gets kicked out of a mental hospital? How much lower could I go?

I'll never forget what one particular administrator/nurse said to me. "Barbara, you really blew it. This was your last chance to have success in your life. I do wish you the best of luck."

She truly didn't believe there was any hope for me. Her feelings were plainly mixed with both pity and scorn. She was actually vocalizing how everyone else felt. I was doomed.

If there was any doubt in my mind concerning my failure and certain misfortune, it was clarified by the staff and patients alike. The whole tone from the patients on the unit about my being kicked out was sympathy and thankfulness that they weren't me. They were still living the good life of opportunity with a team of supportive professionals now and into their future.

This had to be the ultimate rejection, and from the very people who were trained and supposed to be committed to helping me. This was a hospital, a place of healing. They were supposed to release me when I was healthy again, not punish me because I had problems. This was my last chance, and I'd blown it.

But I had no time to dwell on it. I had to focus on procuring living arrangements and fast. They only gave me two weeks. And they weren't helping me. I was completely on my own.

When Francesca brought me to the hospital initially seven months previously, I'd left my car at her house, parked off to the side of their driveway. Soon after, she decided it was too awkward to have to explain to anyone visiting whose car it was and why it was there, so she asked that I have it removed. She was also holding on to some of my money that I had been saving.

Subsequently, my dad in Florida called my uncle Arnold, who lived about ten minutes from Francesca's house, to ask him to pick up my car, money, and other belongings Francesca had in storage. In response to a second call, Uncle Arnold came to my unit ladened with boxes and gave me all of my possessions, money, and much-needed car.

During the two-week period, I hoped that the staff was bluffing. Maybe it was some weird form of therapy. Maybe they really just wanted to break me so I would admit my need for help and be more open to treatment. But that was just another fantasy. This was real. I had totally blown it.

I made some half-hearted attempts to find a place to live, but I guess in the back of my mind I thought if I hadn't found a place after two weeks, they wouldn't just kick me out on the street. The fact is, even in the best of circumstances, it's not easy to get an apartment or a house-share or even a room for rent in two weeks' time.

I asked Francesca if I could go back with her, but too much had changed. I didn't really want to go back, but I was a little desperate. As it turned out, she already had someone staying there, so that wasn't an option. Thank God!

My two weeks were up, and I had no place to go. After saying some last goodbyes, I walked out of the hospital with two staff members who helped me carry my possessions. Then, without lingering for a moment, they left me there on the sidewalk and returned to the unit.

There I was, alone by the parking lot in front of the building. I had one car, six boxes, and nowhere to go.

Looking back, I now know that even in my lowest moment when I felt like an utter failure, God still believed I could have a blessed life. Although there seemed to be nothing left for me, He knew He could use me for something good. His love and power could do anything. "A bruised reed He will not break, and smoking flax He will not quench; He will bring forth justice for truth" (Isaiah 42:3). With God, all things are possible (Mark 10:27).

People will forsake us, but as I learned later, God will never abandon us. At this time, I still refused to accept God into my heart, but now I know that back then at my lowest point of failure, He had not forsaken me, just as He promises in His Word that He will never leave us nor forsake us (Deuteronomy 31:6-8; Joshua 1:5; Hebrews 13:5).

One thing I got from my seven-month stay at that place, and only one thing, was a drug that could stop my fantasizing. That was all they were capable of giving me.

In addition to the humiliation of being kicked out of a mental hospital, I was also suffering from a bad case of bronchitis. The pain in my chest was so severe I went to the ER. Believing I had pneumonia, I asked for an X-ray, which was negative, but the whole ordeal of bronchitis was the final straw. Even though I was not an emotional person, I finally broke down and actually cried. I cried for a full day.

I called Bill. He offered to take me in, but he was living with his parents. I would have had to stay in their unfinished basement, so I declined.

Bill was a born-again believer in Jesus Christ. As a Jewish person, I had been brainwashed not to believe in Jesus. Consequently, just the mention of that name upset me. Making the conditions of our friendship clear, I told him we could be friends only if He didn't talk to me again about Jesus.

Bill had a friend, another born-again believer, who gladly took me in, tears and all, while I was figuring everything out. His idea of giving me a place to live, though, was to have me sleep on his couch in the living room while his wife and three boys continued to live their lives as if I wasn't there.

Shortly thereafter, I found a room for rent in a house in White Plains, New York. Although I had to share the one bathroom and kitchen with three other women, I loved it there. The neighborhood was very pleasant and quiet, and within walking distance to all the stores in the main city of White Plains. I also had free parking behind the house.

The path to a happy, fulfilling life hadn't been found in a unique treatment opportunity. That entire experience was one more thing to add to my list of pursuits that couldn't fill my emptiness, make me happy, or give me a new life.

Deep in my heart, though, I wasn't out of motivation to continue searching. And I wasn't yet out of options to explore.

Chapter 12

FUTILE PURSUITS

FOR THE NEXT FIVE YEARS, I GOT TOGETHER WITH Bill from time to time. He was always there for me when I needed anything—to borrow money, play a little basketball, or if I was feeling down and just wanted company. He didn't force his beliefs on me, but he did respectfully invite me to his church. On a few occasions, when I had nothing to do and was feeling lonely, I went to church with him or to one of his Bible studies. The people there seemed phony and crazy.

Bill was a true friend, with absolutely no ulterior motive but to help me in any way he could, but my calls to him were infrequent. He was quiet and seemed boring.

Within walking distance from where I lived was a grocery store. I applied for a job and was hired in their bakery department. The job was easy enough, but like all the other jobs I had previously dabbled in, it was unbearably boring. Still, I stuck with it for several months.

The bakery supervisor, a woman named Eileen, and I became friends. We hung out together after work, and I got to know her and some of her friends.

Eileen was a lesbian, and she tried to sway me into that lifestyle. I had never considered that way of life. The mere thought of it had always disgusted me. But in spite of my clearly stated feelings about the matter, Eileen pursued me in any subtle way she could. I thought the whole thing was repulsive and shunned her advances.

She was an interesting person, though, and I still enjoyed our friendship, but she never stopped her advances toward me. Over time, our friendship grew. Feeling alone and wanting to be liked and accepted, I was vulnerable.

To my shock, over time, I actually began to fall in love with her. We became intimately involved, and I soon began to appreciate that the gay life held a lot of excitement, passion, and new friends.

We went to Greenwich Village every weekend with another friend, a gay guy, and always had a blast. It was fun being out there, embracing my new identity, and expressing it to a watching world. I was at my prime, about twenty-five, pretty, and had a great body. I felt on top of this game.

We went out dancing at various clubs, and I loved it. I was in my glory. Ignorantly, I believed that the epitome of living was partying and dancing all night and getting back into White Plains at 5:30 the next morning. I never drank, though.

There was also a very dark side to this life. While I was with Eileen, I was very happy, but being dependent on her for my happiness inevitably led to emotional pain.

After she got what she wanted from me—my devotion—she went on to newer quests. Callously, she called me one night to tell me she was with someone else she'd fallen in love with. I had never thought she would ever cheat on me. I'd trusted her to be faithful. I loved her and believed it was mutual. All I'd really been to her from the beginning was just a game to see if she could win me. First, *she* was desperate to have me. Now, *I* was the desperate one.

Her betrayal was too much for me to handle. She'd gone over a line we could never cross back over again. That was my wake-up call. I knew I had to make a choice and fast. I couldn't continue down this crazy road. My heart's desire since I'd been a child was to one day have a husband and children, a boy and a girl. Somehow, I had gotten off track.

I wrote Eileen a letter stating simply that my goal had always been to have a husband and children and that I needed to break it off permanently. I also told her to never call me or contact me again. Fortunately, we no longer worked together since I had quit my previous job with her and was working as a cashier at another grocery store.

Perhaps the letter shocked and upset her, but she didn't contact me. The two years that followed were perhaps the loneliest time of my life, even though our time together had only lasted about eight months. I still had friends to hang out with, but my thoughts were on her.

Immediately after our breakup, to ease the pain of being without her, I went to a few gay clubs in search of another relationship. But after about two months, I was done with that life forever.

What I thought was love had really just been a need-based obsession. Being gay wasn't me. In my vulnerability, I got involved unintentionally with something very wrong for me—another failed path. The gay life was not my avenue to happiness.

During the two years that followed my breakup with Eileen, I immersed myself in working out at the gym and playing racquetball. Also, around this time, it dawned on me that I didn't want to go on working at these boring, dead-end jobs, such as grocery stores, for the rest of my life. Somehow, I needed to find a job I enjoyed and that offered advancement and a future.

I remembered that when I was twenty and ready to leave Linden Hill, the treatment team had come up with a discharge plan that involved vocational training. To me, being normal meant rejecting their plans and breaking off all ties with the mental health scene. In my pride, I had chosen to disassociate from anything pertaining to treatment. Not only had I burned my bridges, but many years had passed. I couldn't possibly go back to them now and get the help they previously offered.

According to the plan I'd rejected, among other things, I was to attend VESID (Vocational and Educational Services for Individuals with Disabilities). Back then, I had wanted nothing to do with VESID.

At this point, though, I was on my own, but I had no career training. I managed to have a good living arrangement on my own, and I still didn't want a therapist, but I desperately needed career skills. I had an associate degree in business, but that hadn't opened up any doors.

So again, I did the unimaginable. I tried to get into VESID. They were located in White Plains within walking distance of where I lived. Walking in there was one of the scariest things I've ever done.

They told me I couldn't just walk in without a referral. Directly across the street was a state-run, out-patient counseling center. I went in and got myself a therapist. After a few weeks of enduring her on a weekly basis, she was willing to give me the referral I needed. It seemed I had come almost full circle with the initial plans that had been made for me some six years earlier.

I began training at VESID Monday through Friday, 9 a.m. to 1 p.m. This particular training was called ICD and involved learning computer basics, word processing, and keyboarding. A big sign on the door read, "International Center for the Disabled." To top it all off, this training center, consisting of two large classrooms, was located within one of the buildings on the Westchester Community College (WCC) campus.

Years ago, that would have bothered me. I would have been mortified to be seen there. But surprisingly, I no longer cared. I wanted a good job. I wanted a chance. I didn't care what the students of WCC might think of me, if they even noticed. I felt that I was more focused on pursuing attainable goals than the people at the college who were working on a two-year degree which may or may not actually get them a job, as my degree had failed to do for me.

At ICD, I eagerly prepared to take a County government civil service exam and a performance typing test. Not knowing anything about County jobs before starting ICD, I found out that they offered career growth, good benefits, an excellent retirement plan, and job security.

Prior to my exam, ICD secured a volunteer internship for me as a clerical office assistant to one of the management staff in the Personnel Department in one of the County office buildings in White Plains, where I was able to become familiar with the County work environment.

After about six months of training, I took and passed my first civil service exam, Intermediate Typist I. I scored fairly well, and since that was an entry level position, it didn't take long to get hired.

I started at a District Office of Social Services in White Plains. I genuinely enjoyed this job. The County atmosphere was different from the private sector. It was more relaxed and less demanding. The work was so much more interesting and rewarding than the previous jobs I'd experienced, and I was good at it. I loved being there, and the people were nice.

I'd finally found a job that I enjoyed, paid well, and offered a future. My goals were being realized. Although I'd been financially free from my parents since living at the Y, I now no longer needed Medicaid or SSI. I had better medical benefits at my job, and my salary was more than sufficient to support me. It was such a great feeling finally being completely financially independent.

As I continued to work at the County, I knew I had the potential to move up within the ranks. I began to take more exams and got promoted twice.

Happily settled into a good job and comfortable routine, and having gotten over Eileen, it seemed a good time to start trying to meet a guy. Although I was busier and feeling much happier with the course of my life, I still felt that familiar longing in my heart that couldn't easily be filled with a worldly accomplishment like pursuing a career.

A husband and a family seemed to be a time-honored and socially acceptable way of finding one's fulfillment in life. Maybe a husband and children would bring my life to completion.

I decided to respond to ads in the singles' section of the local paper. After a period of several months, a common theme began to emerge. After talking on the phone, we'd meet at a restaurant. The guy would usually show interest in me, but relatively quickly, I knew the feeling wasn't mutual. In a few cases, we'd both conclude it wasn't right.

That's not to say there weren't some nice men. Most of them were decent and financially successful, but there was no spark. After years of observing my mother's discontentment as a result of her mistake in marriage, I had vowed never to marry a man unless I loved him. Out of social and financial necessity, she finally agreed to marry a man she didn't love and had been unhappy ever since.

After many nice dinners, I realized the singles scene held no promise, so I moved on. Not meeting the right man had nothing to do with my recent stint in the gay life. I knew in my heart I wasn't gay. Trying to find my soulmate in the single's scene and forcing love when it's not the right time was simply not going to work.

Later, I came to realize that with or without a man in my life, the loneliness I felt in my soul could never be filled by another human being. Being truly complete can only come from knowing and loving God, as Colossians 2:10 says, "You are complete in Him, who is the head of all principality and power."

One day at the mall, I was approached by a nice young couple pitching some type of get-rich-quick program. Their plan, they promised, could make me independently wealthy in only six to eight extra hours of my time per week. It was ideal for someone like me working full-time. All I had to do was sell some products and recruit some new people.

Shortly into our conversation, we sat down as they illuminated their plan. It made perfect sense, and it seemed doable. If I became financially secure to the point of having everything I could ever want or need, and if I never had to work another day in my life, that would be the ultimate happiness.

I knew it wasn't going to be easy, but I was determined to stick with it. I had to sell the products, use the products, and recruit people to work under me who would do the same. But the idea of cold canvass selling had always seemed daunting, and recruiting people I'd never met, even scarier. How would I get over that hurdle?

"That's why we have our meetings," they told me.

At these regularly scheduled seminars, the leaders, who had very successfully gone before us, would build us up (dream building, they called it) with promises of houses, boats, and similar material items. It certainly behooved them to inspire us to succeed since we were all connected to their potential growth in the business.

In their arsenal of training tools, they not only had various motivational rallies to pump us up, but they also had book tables with a vast array of how-to-succeed books. After the first meeting, I found out that the company was Amway. That was okay with me. After that first meeting, I was raring to go. If I did everything according to their timelines, I could in one year's time, they assured me, be making up to $100,000 per year working only part-time. Surely, I could do it in *five* years.

It definitely required a lot of work. I stuck with it, though, for about three years, attending the meetings, using the products, selling some products sporadically, and leaving each meeting with a renewed feeling of hope and determination. Finally, however, I realized this flower of success was never going to bloom.

I've always loved sports. I belonged to a racquetball club where I played a lot. I worked out with weights and cardio machines and got involved in as many sports-related activities as I could. I joined softball teams with the County and also played on a private league. In the winter, I joined a women's basketball team.

I had also been going regularly to a popular singles tennis night every Saturday close to where I lived. I wasn't looking for anyone. I just loved tennis. I even played doubles outside, and as a fill-in inside with a group of older ladies.

Playing sports turned out to be an enjoyable escape. Unlike other pursuits, it had its health benefits too. Although having good health and enjoying fun sports is a good thing, it never brought me any spiritual fulfillment. To try to reach that goal with these pastimes was an exercise in futility. I always left feeling alone and empty.

Since my parents' love had come only in material form, they had always yielded to my every tangible want. They had never told me no, especially when it came to junk food, which included the sugary kind. I had never had any limits. Five brownies were just as permissible as one.

Being the self-indulgent person I was brought up to be, treating myself was second nature. Many a night I would take refuge in an unhealthful meal, and of course, an even more decadent dessert.

Food was the perfect escape. Because I was young, worked out, and played sports, I could eat as much as I wanted, within reason, and not gain weight. Obviously, food was never going to lift my spirits permanently. At best, it was a temporary, nightly joy, which could only provide a brief, pleasurable escape.

For ten years, since the age of twenty, I had tried everything I could possibly think of that held any remote promise of giving me joy, a sense of purpose, or hope for something more out of life. Aside from getting into drugs or alcohol, which thank God I had no interest in, I didn't know what else to try.

Over these years, I had pursued anything and everything I could think of—religions, philosophy, materialism, a career, relationships—nothing seemed to offer any sustained value or fulfillment. Materially, I had achieved most of my goals, and I felt somewhat content. To anyone I came in contact with, I portrayed a joyful person. I was happy on the surface, but beneath that exterior, I felt alone and empty.

After having searched out all the possible avenues I could think of that might offer something real and meaningful, I pondered the fact that my ten-year search had yielded absolutely nothing. With nothing else left to look into, I decided to try something I hadn't been willing to consider before.

PART IV
THE REDEEMED LIFE

Chapter 13

THE TRUTH

WHILE TAKING A WALK AROUND MY NEIGHBORHOOD and thinking that there was nothing left to try that might fill the void in my heart, I began to reflect on what Bill had been trying to tell me for the previous five years about Jesus. I had adamantly refused to listen.

Now, I thought, *why not try Jesus?*

As I was walking, I said a little prayer in my heart. "Jesus, if You're real, please show me." That was it. I didn't pour out my heart or even ask for forgiveness. I didn't understand that I needed forgiveness. Actually, I didn't even know if He was real.

Being Jewish, I was totally ignorant about Christianity. I didn't understand that people were sinners. I didn't even know what the Gospel was or what salvation meant. But God was faithful to my little prayer, simple as it was.

With the same zeal and enthusiasm I had had for all my other endeavors, I became excited about this too. Immediately, I went home and called Bill. "I'm a Christian now," I told him.

Very happy about my decision, Bill took me to a Messianic congregation (Jewish believers in Jesus Christ as their Messiah). To find one, we had to travel to Lodi, New Jersey, to a congregation called Beth Israel. The place was huge. Hundreds of people, both Jewish and non-Jewish believers in Jesus filled the seats.

The pastor/rabbi was a young Jewish man, Jonathan Cahn, who later became the New York Times best-selling author of

The Harbinger. He now has a book series based on that first intriguing book.

This congregation seemed to be a place for new believers. The teaching at Beth Israel was straight from the Bible and revealed the truth about God, His love, and the answers I'd been seeking. Pastor Jonathan taught that I could have a personal relationship with God. How incredible was that?

All of the basics were being taught. Perfect for me! I was happy to learn such incredible truths that were new to me. What a revelation to learn that I was a sinner. After my "turning point" at twenty, I'd thought I was a truly good person.

Pastor Jonathan pointed out that, like me, many people hold fast to the conviction that although they aren't perfect, they're still good people. They rely on the good things they do to get them into heaven, not understanding the Bible teaches that our good deeds are as "filthy rags" in God's sight (Isaiah 64:6). No one can be good enough to go to heaven.

I learned that God created a perfect, sinless world, but Adam and Eve disobeyed God and sin entered God's perfect creation. The Old Testament shows the downward spiral of humankind that resulted from the introduction of sin. No one is able to obey God's commandments perfectly, and sin cuts us off from God. Our inability to obey the Ten Commandments makes us aware of our desperate need for a Savior. The Old Testament also gives us hope through its prophecies of a coming Lamb of God who would take away the sins of the world.

Romans 3:23 says, "All have sinned and fall short of the glory of God." The word translated *sin* is an archery term meaning "to miss the mark—the bull's eye." Romans 6:23 tells us God's remedy: "For the wages of sin is death, but the gift of God is eternal life in Christ Jesus our Lord." What is that gift of God? John 3:16 shows us God's gift: "God so loved the world that He gave His only begotten Son, that whoever believes in Him should not perish but have everlasting life." Jesus is the final sacrificial "Lamb of God who takes away the sin of the world!" (John 1:29).

When I understood my sinful state, I confessed my sins to Jesus in prayer and thanked Him for dying for me and for saving me. I opened up my heart to accept Jesus as the Lord of my life and began to talk to God in prayer. My life began to change radically as God worked in my heart. That I began to have a real, personal relationship with the Creator of the universe was the most joyful thing imaginable.

From reading the Bible and attending the weekly services at Beth Israel, I began to know God more and more each day. I had finally found the truth about the love of God and my purpose in life—just what I had been longing for all those years.

I had asked Jesus to show me if He was real, and He did. In my joy and wonder, I was free to begin a new and exciting life discovering the awesomeness and power of the one and only true God.

As I began to pray to God in Jesus' name, He actually answered each one of my prayers—even the daily, seemingly unimportant ones. Whenever I asked Him for help, He answered faithfully. It doesn't get more real than that!

As a child, I had prayed to God. In my childhood anguish and despair, I'd even written Him letters, but He hadn't helped me, or so I thought. Now, I finally understood why. My sin had separated me from Him. "But your iniquities have separated you from your God; and your sins have hidden His face from you, so that He will not hear" (Isaiah 59:2). Now that I had accepted His Son, who paid the price for my sins, I had access to God.

Only after I accepted Jesus, who is the Bridge that closes the gap between me, a sinner, and a holy God, was I finally able to have a relationship with God. Because Jesus paid the price for my sin, and I had accepted Him as my Savior and Lord, my sins were forgiven.

Of course, I'm not sinless. Everyone sins, including Christians. The difference with regard to sin between believers in Jesus Christ and non-believers is the fact that believers' sins are forgiven because we have accepted God's provision for our sin—the atoning death of His perfect Son, Jesus Christ.

God met me right where I was. Even though I didn't confess my sins at that time, He was faithful to answer my little prayer to show me if He was real. All I did was reach out to Him in prayer and call on His powerful name. John 1:12 promises, "But as many as received Him, to them He gave the right to become children of God, to those who believe in His name." James 4:8 says, "Draw near to God and He will draw near to you," and that is exactly what God did when I said that little prayer.

As I read the Bible, I learned that God was always faithful to His people, the Israelites, to give back to them what their mistakes and sin had caused them to lose. On one occasion, when their sin put them in a dismal state, a plague of locusts devoured all their crops. Despite the fact that they had brought their problems on themselves, when they repented, God lovingly made up for those lost years and blessed them. In Joel 2:25, God said to His people, "So I will restore to you the years that the swarming locust has eaten…." By God's love and mighty hand in my life, He more than restored the "locust years" of my life.

Depression Redeemed

After being depressed for so many years, it's not surprising that God redeemed that part of my life first. Joy became the new theme of my life. Galatians 5:22 says that one of the attributes of the fruit of the Spirit is joy. With God's Spirit within me, supernatural joy began to permeate my life. Regardless of what happens, my inner joy prevails because I can always go to Him for help, and He never fails to answer (Psalms 46:1, Hebrews 4:16)

I no longer have to go through each day wondering, "What's the point?" Jesus was not just a new religion. I'd checked out too many belief systems and tried too hard to make them work to know that this wasn't like any of the former array of religions I had tried to convince myself to believe.

Those other religions couldn't help because they were man-made. Christianity is not a man-made religion. It's not a religion at all; it's a relationship with God. The depression is gone because I now have an enduring hope, a new life and purpose, and I look forward to an even better life for all eternity.

Trust Redeemed

The day I accepted Jesus into my heart, I was a mess, selfish and unloving. Yet, He loved and accepted me just as I was. In His mercy and love, however, He didn't leave me that way. He immediately went to work cleaning up my life and healing the wounds of my past.

Trust was a big issue for me. One thing my parents and life had taught me was that I could trust no one. My father had continually hurt me emotionally so I couldn't depend on him for emotional support. I projected that onto God. My father never kept his promises, nor did he even consider that practice to be wrong so I saw God as not trustworthy. Since my father criticized me on a regular basis, I thought God was critical of me too.

God is nothing like my father, but I dared not trust anyone, not even God. Of course, my Heavenly Father understood my issue with trust. In my brokenness, He proved His faithfulness to me by answering my prayers and changing my heart and life. As a result, I learned to trust Him a little more each day. Now, I trust God one hundred percent. I know He'll never let me down, and I can never lose His love (see Romans 8:38-39).

My Education Redeemed

When I accepted Jesus, I was renting a room in a house in White Plains, New York, and working for Westchester County as a secretary. Although I had taken more civil service exams and was promoted twice (from Typist to Office Assistant to Secretary), I had gone as far as I could within my department without a bachelor's degree.

Working in the Department of Social Services (DSS), I observed my coworkers who were Eligibility Examiners, who interviewed the clients to determine their eligibility for services. That position seemed more professional than my job, and I aspired to do that. It paid more and held more responsibility, but it required a bachelor's degree.

Believing it was God's will that I go back to school, I enrolled in an accelerated degree program at Concordia College in Bronxville, New York, and took out a loan to pay. I could earn my degree in two years part-time. The requirements for getting into this program were to have two years of college credits and be working full-time. I met those conditions.

Because it was a condensed program, the course load was equivalent to attending college full-time for two years. I also had to take a prerequisite course at Westchester Community College and two additional courses at Mercy College at the end of the program, which added two full traditional semesters to the total time to get my bachelor's degree. God was faithful to give me the strength to complete my degree.

A Home Redeemed

Sharing a house was no longer a practical living situation. I needed to be in my own place before going back to school. I knew God was leading me when someone at work told me about a studio apartment he was living in and how nice and affordable it was. After we played basketball one night, he showed me his apartment. I was astonished at how spacious and beautiful it was. And the rent was reasonable.

I didn't want to make a move outside the will of God, but seeing that place was the confirmation I needed to overcome my indecisiveness. I immediately got my name on the waiting list.

In a few weeks, I signed a lease for a studio apartment at a place called the Amberlands in Croton-on-Hudson, New York, with a million-dollar view overlooking the Hudson River. My place was perfect for me and incredibly peaceful. Bill and a friend from church helped me move.

For many years out on my own, not having adequate finances, I'd had to move from one less than ideal living arrangement to another. To have to pick up and move so often was difficult. As I settled into this new apartment, I knew God had redeemed those horrible moving and living experiences by giving me this beautiful, sunny, tranquil apartment.

My first evening there, as I lay on my bed listening to praise music while looking out through the glass door of my apartment high up on a hill, I could see the sun set behind the distant mountains with its array of colors glistening off the Hudson River. God bestowed that breathtaking view on me, I believe, as a housewarming gift that I could enjoy every day. He'd brought me to a place I could really love. As I praised the Lord, I felt an amazing peace in that apartment.

My Insecurity Redeemed

My next challenge was to handle full-time school along with my full-time job. Logistically I was all set to return to college, but after so many years of being out of school, I was a bit nervous about going back. I decided to major in psychology, which had always fascinated me, in spite of, or maybe because of, my upbringing.

The seven students who started together would stay together throughout the entire two years. Since it was a condensed program, we only took one course at a time, shorter than a traditional school class but with tons of homework crammed into it.

We were required to attend class for four hours every Tuesday night, from 6:00 to 10:00 p.m., and one Saturday a month, from 9:00 a.m. to 1:00 p.m. We had to write at least one paper a week, take tests almost every week, and read several books at a time. My goal was set before me, and I was determined to succeed.

I focused intently on succeeding, but I was so lacking in self-confidence that each time I wrote a paper or was about to take a test, I would pray to God to help me to just pass. I really worked hard, but all I thought I could manage and all I prayed for was to pass. Yet, each and every paper, test, or grade I got back was an A.

Being called stupid every day of my life growing up, I still believed it to some extent even at this point. As I consistently received straight A's, I began to stand out in our group to the deans. (I never told my classmates my grades.) God was redeeming that haunting insecurity that all my life had made me believe I was stupid.

As busy as I was with working and going to school, I noticed that what I learned in one thirty-minute sermon every Friday evening at Beth Israel was more life-changing than all I learned in the long hours in college classes and studying at home. I realized that being smart had absolutely nothing to do with how well I could memorize information, pass a test, or put together a good essay. That's just knowledge. Wisdom, on the other hand, can only come from being connected to God, and true wisdom always *produces* something for His glory.

One day God is going to ask me how I used the gifts He has given me. Did my gifts yield something of value? Or did I waste them on prideful gain or with selfish motives. I believe that answer is determined by how much I've loved and helped others as God's power and wisdom guided me.

James 3:17 sums it up this way: "But the wisdom that is from above is first pure, then peaceable, gentle, willing to yield, full of mercy and good fruits, without partiality and without hypocrisy." *Full of good fruits* means we are to produce the work that God has planned for us to do which is always to glorify Him and help others.

My Character Redeemed

Working and going to school full-time was indeed very demanding and stressful. Yet, the amazing thing was, as I continued to spend time with the Lord in prayer daily, I came up with a schedule that helped me organize my time and handle the extra demands more smoothly. I know God guided me in coming up with this schedule because previously I'd never had any skills in time-management or self-discipline.

In addition to my Monday to Friday, nine-to-five work schedule, I went to school on Tuesday nights and spent Thursday nights studying. I went to the gym after work on Mondays, Wednesdays, and Fridays. Friday nights after my workout, I went to Beth Israel. They had a Friday night as well as Sunday morning service. The Friday night service after the health club worked perfectly, leaving my weekends free.

On weekend mornings, I devoted four hours to studying, writing papers, et cetera. After 1:00 p.m. on Saturdays and Sundays, my time was completely free. No chaos. Although demanding, I stayed the course and didn't quit.

On top of that burdensome schedule, I actually managed to read the entire Bible in a year. Wanting to put God first, I decided to follow a schedule to read the Bible from Genesis to Revelation in a year. Unlike school, reading my Bible was relaxing and enjoyable.

Having two-and-a-half years in front of me with the constant stress of a full-time job and full-time school was still overwhelming. With no breaks as in a traditional semester, I scarcely had time to breathe. It was definitely a lot of work, but I refused to give up.

Through this experience, all of the vital character traits I'd never been taught—self-discipline, perseverance, self-confidence, time-management—were effectively redeemed.

During my time of hard work, God didn't just give me a great schedule. He provided even more than I could ever have hoped for or imagined.

Chapter 14

THE GIFT OF LOVE

I WASN'T LOOKING FOR A BOYFRIEND AT THIS TIME. My focus was on completing my degree, working at the County, going to church, and working out at the gym. I had no time for a social life unless someone could fit into *my* schedule. My constant joy was my growing relationship with the Lord and learning all I could about Him. Besides that, I had friends at church, and all of my needs were met.

A Christian friend, Suzette, invited me to spend New Year's Eve at her apartment. I'd met her at a Christian concert I'd attended with Bill, and we immediately became friends. She was going to spend New Year's Eve at home with her boyfriend, Jeff, and his brother, Andy, to just hang out, eat, and watch movies. She warned me that Andy tended to use bad language, but I decided not to allow that to prevent me from spending the holiday with friends. Besides, who was I to judge?

Suzette's apartment was near where I lived, so I wouldn't have to travel far on a night when drunken drivers could be out on the roads. Otherwise, I would have gone to my church in Lodi, New Jersey, an hour away, since they had something planned there for the holiday.

When I arrived at her apartment and met her boyfriend, Jeff, and his brother, Andy, I noticed Andy appeared angry about something. He seemed to have a chip on his shoulder.

Through conversation, Andy and I realized that we were both going to the same gym. By coincidence, we were also both working in White Plains at a government job.

We all had a pleasant time talking, eating, and laughing. We watched a movie I'd brought, *Lord of the Flies*, which we all enjoyed. Since I had to read that book for school, I took advantage of the long night to watch it. After saying good-bye and driving home, I didn't give Andy a second thought.

A few days into the new year, Suzette called to tell me that the next time I saw Andy at the gym, I should say hello and ask him to grab some dinner after our workout.

"Why?" I asked.

"Just do it," she said.

She was a more seasoned Christian and a trusted friend, so I took her advice. Not a big deal. The very next time I saw Andy at the gym, which was usually packed at the time we went after work, I asked him if he wanted to grab a bite after our workout sometime.

"Sure!" he said. We made plans for the next time we'd both be working out.

I wasn't interested in a man at this time, least of all him. I was focused on school, very happy and fulfilled, and too busy.

Andy was living in White Plains with his parents in their apartment. The thought of dating him never entered my mind, but if it had, it wouldn't have been a pleasant thought. He was very rough around the edges, wore cowboy boots, wore his hair long, and had an earring in one ear.

Andy and I went to a Mexican restaurant directly across the street from the gym. During our conversation, I invited him to go to church with me. At first he told me, "No, I don't think so." Then, toward the end of the meal, he reconsidered and said he would go.

I found out later that the only reason he had decided to go to church with me was because he thought he would score with me in bed. Not knowing his intentions at the time, I still didn't feel comfortable driving an hour with a man I didn't know to the Friday evening service I usually attended.

Instead, we drove to Lodi, New Jersey, in my car to the Sunday morning service at Beth Israel. I was a bit disappointed because the regular pastor, who was very dynamic and funny, wasn't there so someone else was giving the message. This young Jewish man, however, had a story to tell about his past that Andy could relate to.

Andy is Italian and was brought up attending the Catholic Church, yet this Jewish man reached him that morning. At the end of the message, as was customary, the preacher asked if anyone wanted to ask Jesus into their heart. He prayed out loud, and then he asked anyone who had made that decision to raise their hand, saying that someone would take them aside, talk to them, and give them a Bible.

I looked over at Andy, sitting right next to me. He was crying. I couldn't believe it! Andy's heart was open, and he accepted the Lord. He left his seat to talk with someone. I was definitely surprised, but happy. I met up with him a short time later, and we headed out. He was very excited about what had just happened to him. After church that morning, we went to lunch to celebrate Andy's accepting the Lord into his heart.

Apparently, a couple of weeks earlier, Andy had been crying out to God for help. In a bad relationship for many years, he had been severely hurt emotionally. He and his girlfriend had broken up several months prior, but he couldn't seem to get over her, even though he knew she didn't love him and treated him badly. As hard as he tried, he couldn't seem to shake his obsession with her.

One night in the parking lot of his parents' apartment building, he literally cried his heart out to God, loudly and uncontrollably. In his car that night he'd prayed that God would take that girl out of his head and send him a woman he could love and have a family with.

Many times before, Andy had looked out of his parents' apartment window at the Roman Catholic Church next door. He wanted to get close to God, but he couldn't seem to bring himself to go back to that church because he'd had an unpleasant experience with the Catholic Church in general.

Incredibly, right after Andy accepted the Lord into his heart, that miserable obsession he'd had for so many years with his ex-girlfriend finally disappeared. He was noticeably transformed in other areas as well. He no longer cursed. The anger was gone, and his countenance looked joyful.

Andy had had problems with alcohol. He would drink himself into a stupor almost every night and barely stagger into his parents' apartment to sleep. He also smoked pot and did drugs fairly regularly. From the moment he accepted Jesus into his heart, he completely stopped drinking and doing drugs. He had what Christians would call an immediate conversion experience. Indeed, I could see he was a new person with a new hope that radiated joy. Soon, Andy got rid of the earring, the cowboy boots, and the long hair.

About two weeks after that Sunday, he called me at work to tell me that he was moving out of his parents' apartment and into my apartment complex in Croton-on-Hudson just two buildings over from mine—a short walking distance away. I found it odd that he was moving so close to me after having known me for only two weeks, but I was glad to have a friend there.

A week after he moved into my complex, he told me he was in love with me and that I was the one he wanted to spend the rest of his life with. I explained to him that I just wanted to be friends.

Our friendship was good. The months that followed were really fun. He cooked for me almost every night and did anything he could think of to help me get through the drudgeries of work and school. He even helped with my laundry. It seemed that pleasing me was his life's focus. He would do anything to make my life easier.

As a Custodian at the White Plains City School District, later to become the Head Custodian, Andy managed to get a computer from the school and set it up in my apartment. When

I was preparing for a presentation, he borrowed an overhead projector so I could practice my presentation at home.

For another class, he made a really colorful, laminated chart to display data I'd collected for another presentation. I was truly the envy of my classmates that day. They must have wondered how in the world I had time to make such an elaborate display.

Andy's life seemed to revolve around me. He lavished me with love. Every holiday was a reason for him to surprise me with flowers, a gift, or a special dinner. I never took advantage of him, though. The old me before knowing the Lord might have, but now I placed my trust in God. I was committed to honoring Him.

While I didn't love Andy romantically, I had a great time with him as a friend. He was the only person who could actually make me laugh uncontrollably.

Spending time together in Croton was an amazing experience. We truly enjoyed each other's company and the small pleasures of life. We went to the gym together after work. Every Saturday and Sunday morning, Andy would anxiously wait for me to finish my four hours of schoolwork. After that, we were free to enjoy the rest of the day together.

We spent most of our time doing healthful activities such as biking, tennis, basketball, and walking. On weekend evenings, we'd rent a video, and I'd walk over to his apartment with a big bowl of popcorn.

Every night, he would walk me home from his building to mine, and with heartfelt sincerity, say the same thing, "Barbara, I really love you. Will you marry me?" And every night, with a heavy heart, I would tell him the same thing. "Please stop asking me. I don't love you that way. I just want to be friends."

Our friendship was very special, but I just wasn't able to trust him enough to marry him. I couldn't help but think that all of his advances were just a con act to win me over.

After almost a year of being friends, the realization finally hit me. Andy genuinely loved me. His actions proved it. When I knew he was sincere, I decided the next time he asked me to marry him, I would say yes. Since he asked me nearly every night, all I had to do was wait for the next time. As expected, he did. When I said yes, he was shocked.

We decided not to get married until after I finished school in another year. Being engaged, we enjoyed a truly memorable time in beautiful Croton-on-Hudson. We'd often sit on a bench at our favorite park by the water, watching the sun set while we talked and held hands. Wanting to honor God, we remained abstinent until our wedding night.

Andy, by nature, and also because of the loving mother he had, is a very loving, thoughtful, and nurturing man. He needed a woman he could take care of. His heart's desire is, and probably always will be, to make me happy and to pamper me unselfishly with his love.

God knew exactly what I needed. He sent the right man to me when I was extremely stressed and needed a helping friend. God gave me Andy, knowing I needed that extra love. God knew exactly how to redeem my loveless childhood by sending me a man uniquely gifted to love and care for me, one whose heart He had prepared just for me.

The biggest deficit in my life, love, was powerfully redeemed. "Now to Him who is able to do exceedingly abundantly above all that we ask or think, according to the power that works in us, to Him be glory in the church by Christ Jesus to all generations, forever and ever. Amen" (Ephesians 3:20-21).

Another thing God redeemed were my years growing up having no one who took the time or effort to cook for me. In my house growing up, breakfast was boxed cereal, which we got for ourselves. For lunch during the week, we were given money to buy school lunches. Dinners were prepared for the sole purpose of pleasing one person only—the man of the house, who worked hard and expected to come home to a good meal.

Of course, that's not a bad thing, but the only meat my dad wanted almost every night was beef in one form or another—pot roast, brisket, steak, roast beef, et cetera. I never liked beef because I had a difficult time chewing and swallowing it.

Vegetables always came out of a can. On weekends, we didn't have a formal breakfast or lunch, only brunch prepared for Dad. If we didn't like it, we had to fend for ourselves until dinner.

My mom never made me something I liked for dinner. I just ate cereal. My dad would go into his spiel about how I had the audacity to eat cereal when my mother made such a nice dinner, not caring that he made me feel guilty.

I know God intentionally restored that part of my life with a husband who is not only a great cook, but who enjoys preparing meals just for me. Andy still does all of the cooking in our house, and he never seems to tire of preparing something special for me almost every night.

To my amazement, God had already redeemed my life in reverse. He prepared me in advance for what He knew I would have to go through later. Of course, God knows the end before it happens because He is eternal and not limited by time and space. He gifted me socially, emotionally, intellectually, and with a strong mind.

I was too young to remember, but I've been told I used to walk up to strangers and just start talking to them. I had no fear of people back then. I simply enjoyed conversing with everyone. Although that gift was badly damaged during my childhood years, it's a gift I'll always possess. Over the years, it has been recovered, but I much prefer to use it to glorify God by talking to people about Jesus.

I recall that as a child I used to playact for my parents. My emotions were intense, and I could cry at will effortlessly. They thought I was nuts, and my drama days quickly disappeared.

Due to my emotionally abusive childhood, my profound depression and addictive behavior could only be described as normal under the circumstances. I recovered from all of that only because I found joy in the reality of my Lord and because of His power to change me. God gifted me with a strong mind.

The fact that I didn't become psychotic in such a household attests to that fact.

This shows God's awesome sovereignty in lovingly preparing each one of us in advance, in perhaps more ways than we may ever be aware of, to handle the struggles He knows we will face.

It would be impossible to recount the innumerous ways God has radically redeemed my painful past. Ultimately, however, the best redemption I could ever hope for or imagine is beyond anything that could happen in this brief lifetime. He has redeemed my life from His eternal, justified wrath on sin so that I can be with Him forever, experiencing complete joy for all eternity!

> "He who believes in the Son has everlasting life; and he who does not believe the Son shall not see life, but the wrath of God abides on him" (John 3:36). Not only does He save us from His wrath, God promises to "show me the path of life; in Your presence is fullness of joy; at Your right hand are pleasures forevermore" (Psalms 16:11).

Andy and I continued to attend Beth Israel for a while longer, but we eventually decided to switch to a church closer to us, a small messianic congregation, Light of Israel, in Yonkers, New York. The congregation consisted of about twenty-five of us, if everyone showed up simultaneously. We became close friends with the pastor and his wife, Rich and Julia, both Jewish believers in Jesus.

We asked Pastor Rich to marry us, which he was happy to do, provided we go through premarital counseling with him, which he expected of any couple he planned to marry. Although it seemed unnecessary to us at the time, we didn't hesitate to meet with him the required number of times.

I received my bachelor's degree in Psychology in May 1997, and Andy and I were married that June. Suzette, my best friend at the time who had introduced us, served as my bridesmaid. (Incidentally, my friend, Bill, who had led me to the Lord, was married a month before us.)

Andy and I honeymooned for a week at the Sagamore Hotel on Lake George, fully paid for by my mom. We also vacationed a week in Florida to spend time with her. She and Andy hit it off well. We stayed at her condo and visited my brother, Adam, who lived just around the corner with his wife and their seven-year-old son. It was a pleasant, restful week for us swimming, shopping, and eating out a lot with my mom.

My dad had passed away with lung cancer several years earlier. He never saw the point of going to the doctor unless he was actually sick. As a result, he only made a doctor's appointment to determine the cause of his unexpected, severe back pain. By that time, it was discovered that his lung cancer had metastasized to his bones. Following his diagnosis, he declined rapidly and died two months later.

My brother had called to tell me Dad was nearing the end and that I should get down to Florida soon, or it would be too late to see him one last time.

Seeing my dad was a shock. He was just skin and bones. I truly would not have known it was him had I not been told. With his excessively gaunt face, he somehow looked more real to me, maybe because he no longer appeared threatening. His condescending veneer was gone, forced away by disease. There is solace in knowing that I was there with him once more before he died. I truly pray that he called out to Jesus before he passed into eternity.

Since Andy and I both had studio apartments in Croton-on-Hudson, we decided after we married, he would move into my studio. Having finally finished school, it felt strange to have so much time on my hands. I was only working full-time. I had no more classes or homework to worry about, and we no longer had to walk back and forth to each other's apartments.

A dream I'd had since I was young was to one day have children of my own, specifically, a boy and a girl. I knew what young children needed. I had longed for it all my life. I desired to give my children the love I never had. God, in His love and graciousness, fulfilled that desire of my heart. Four months after Andy and I were married, I became pregnant. We were ecstatic, but we suddenly needed to move out of our studio quickly.

Understandably, I experienced many uncertainties about this baby growing inside me. I knew I didn't have any genetic mental illness. My depression had been the result of the way I was raised. My brother, who also had problems, was adopted from a different family than I. But since I was adopted and knew nothing about my biological parents, I was a bit worried. I didn't know their medical history, and had no idea what they even looked like.

To add to my worries, I had been born prematurely and had required an incubator. Would my baby also be premature? Would my pregnancy be normal? Would my baby be normal?

Chapter 15

Two Blessings from Above

I KNEW I WANTED TO BE A STAY-AT-HOME MOM, SO I quickly signed up for a correspondence course in medical transcription so I could work part-time from home. I completed the course during my pregnancy while still working at the County.

After taking my maternity leave, I submitted my resignation at work. I felt strongly that I needed to spend those early years with my child. It didn't make sense to me to have a child and then give her to someone else all day.

Being pregnant was one of the most wonderful times I've ever experienced. It was exciting, scary, and new. Having no symptoms to speak of, I was able to enjoy it. Andy, somehow, had many symptoms. He suffered from nausea, weight gain, and even strange food cravings.

With the same sense of focus and discipline I'd had about school and exercise, I committed myself to the health and care of my baby. While pregnant, I ate perfectly, continued to exercise, and even read to my baby. It was clear to Andy and me that God was blessing this pregnancy. Since it was always my heart's desire to have a boy and a girl, I had already decided on the names, Sarah and David.

Finally, that special moment came. I was ten days past my due date, a fact that worried Andy, but I didn't think it was a problem; neither did the doctors. I felt peace and joy about everything. We wanted the gender to be a surprise, so we grabbed one pink and one blue blanket to take with us to the hospital.

My labor took eight hours—not fun. Then out came Sarah. I realized then that God was fully aware of my previous worries about the normalcy of my baby because I'll never forget what followed.

When Sarah was delivered and the doctor held her up, a clear and almost tangible, prolonged moment of silence ensued. For that moment in time, I saw everyone in the room stop and look at Sarah in clear astonishment at how beautiful she was. Even looking messy from the birth process, her beauty was undeniable.

When she was finally brought to me, all cleaned up, I was overwhelmed all over again with her exquisite face. I couldn't believe it. I'm not just saying that because she was my baby. Babies are usually wrinkly and groggy. Sarah was alert. Her eyes would fix on me. There in the hospital bed together, her tiny body all wrapped up in a blanket, it was like she was staring me down, looking at me and wondering if she could trust me.

How could I be a good mother to her? I wondered.

At church I became known as the lady with the beautiful baby. People in stores would look at Sarah and tell me how beautiful she was. At playgrounds and playgroups, we were instantly popular. God put to rest my worries about having a normal child. Nothing about Sarah was abnormal. She was remarkably beautiful and extremely intelligent. My baby was a delight to play with and take care of.

On two separate occasions, my mom, having taken a special liking to Andy and seeing the change in me since my commitment to Jesus, made a point of flying up to New York to spend a week with us to see the baby.

Not wanting to get into an argument with her during her stay, I delicately described my salvation experience and what

God had done for me. Even though she saw a big change in me, she wasn't willing to accept Jesus as her Savior. In fact, shortly after returning home, she called to tell me that although it was great what my religion had done for me, I shouldn't try to sway other people to my beliefs. No doubt she had gotten those thoughts from Adam.

When Sarah was three, my mother passed away. She died in her sleep at the age of eighty-nine. It was inconclusive as to whether she died of a stroke or heart attack. I only hope that before she died, she made peace with God by accepting His Son as it says in Romans 10:9, "If you confess with your mouth the Lord Jesus and believe in your heart that God has raised Him from the dead, you will be saved."

My parents left Adam and me a good sum of money that enabled Andy and me to move out of our apartment and into a house farther north, from Westchester County into Dutchess County, New York. We decided to pick out our church before we picked our house. Having heard good things about Fishkill Baptist Church, we visited several times and loved it. Sitting behind us our first time there was a real estate agent. We became friends, and she helped us find our first home.

About seven months after we moved into our first house, we had another child, David. I now had my heart's desire—a girl and a boy. I decided to give up working part-time from home as a medical transcriptionist to take care of the kids and the house. Despite the financial burden of giving up my salary, I'll never regret my decision to be home for my children when they were young.

During those years at home, about seven all together, I became very active in our church in the nursery, teaching Sunday school, and leading Pioneer Girls, which Sarah was in. Not working, I also had the luxury of going to the weekly morning moms' group at church. I was able to stay connected to other believers and was always involved in a weekly Bible study group. Being home with my kids, free to take them to the playground a lot and enjoy them as they grew, made those years truly memorable.

Before David was born, it was so nice to wake up with Sarah and have the whole day ahead of us to do whatever we wanted. Most days, I would pack a lunch, and we'd go to one of the nearby playgrounds. During the winters, I made a point of taking Sarah to some of the local playgroups in the area each week. At two, Sarah went to a preschool twice a week where the parents stayed in an adjoining room. We had so many great years together swimming, playing ball, doing crafts, and playing inside games together.

When Sarah was four, David came along. Sarah went off to kindergarten the following year. Watching the bus drive off the first time as Sarah waved to me through the window was one of the most difficult things I've experienced as a mom. I didn't want age five to come so soon for my baby girl.

David was also a pleasure. He was all boy, and I enjoyed many years with him, playing with Matchbox cars, wrestling, and various sports. He wasn't the type to sit for long periods of play like Sarah. He wanted to move and go. Sarah and David had their moments of sibling rivalry, but David adored Sarah, and the two of them could play for hours very well together.

I enjoyed the boy in David. We played every sport imaginable, and even made up our own. Outside or in the house, we threw and kicked a ball around. If David was good all day, we would have our routine wrestling match that night.

We lived in a large townhouse community, so they had many friends to play with. We also had access to Sylvan Lake, which was beautiful and clean, and made our summers great. Every year Sarah had a beach party at the lake for her birthday and a slumber party to follow with a group of her schoolfriends. By God's grace, and my prayers, every one of Sarah's birthday parties at the lake was a perfect, sunny day.

I truly enjoyed spending time with Sarah and David, doing everything together during my stay-at-home years. We spent most days with my best friend and her kids or with my children's friends in our neighborhood after school and on weekends, or together just the three of us—biking, swimming, watching Disney videos, playing board games. It was a blessing.

God had blessed me abundantly. In the previous seven years, since accepting the Lord into my heart, I had earned my BA, married the man of my dreams, bought our first house, had two beautiful children, and became active in our church. God is good!

Although I enjoyed being a stay-at-home mom, eventually, due to the financial stress, Andy and I decided it was time for me to go back to work. At this time, Sarah was seven and David was three. I no longer had a County job to go back to since I had resigned, but I realized from my church volunteer experience that I really enjoyed working with children, so I decided to look for a job teaching at a Christian preschool.

Believing that was the kind of work I was led to do, I applied to various Christian preschools. I really gave this pursuit my all. My résumé was good, and I was prayerful during the entire job search process, but I couldn't find any job openings.

Then a friend told me about a position that had opened up in a Christian preschool not too far from where I lived. She knew someone who worked there and recommended me. Many people at my church were praying for me to get this particular job. It seemed to be a good fit for me, and I really wanted it.

When I went on the interview, though, I was surprised to discover that there was no opening for my son to attend, and the job seemed difficult and overwhelming, not something I would like. I'd been so sure about that job. I had walked through that open door the Lord had provided. I knew He was with me, yet nothing at a preschool had materialized. That avenue was closed.

To bring in a little money the previous year, I had tried substitute teaching sporadically and liked it, so I decided to register with two school districts to ensure I would get enough work. That June, I did all the paperwork and was all set to start subbing the upcoming fall. In hopes of getting a steadier job as a teacher's assistant, should that position become available at a later time, I also sent my résumé to many local schools.

A school position would enable me to be home for Sarah when she got off the bus, but I needed to find daycare for David. I researched the nearby daycare facilities and finally chose the best one. David was all set to start.

Naturally, paying for daycare would be an added expense. When I subtracted the cost of daycare from my projected income, I wasn't going to make a lot, but it was at least something. Having been out of the workforce for so long, I was very excited to start my new work venture and eagerly looked forward to the fall.

Then one evening at my weekly Bible study, someone told me I should try a summer job as a camp counselor at one of the local day camps before I started to work in the fall. They said it would be fun, my kids would go free, and I would bring in some much-needed money.

All of that sounded good, so I followed through on that idea. Thank God I did. I would never have known what the Lord had for me had I not faithfully walked through every open door He provided. He was faithful to close a door if it was wrong for me.

I looked in the local paper and found an ad recruiting counselors for a summer camp nearby. At the interview, I discovered it was a daycare center, and the owner, Carol, was hiring for their Summer camp program. She was very nice and told me she'd get back to me.

A couple of weeks later, Carol called me. She was in a jam. Her Program Director had given her two weeks' notice, and Carol was leaving soon for her annual three-week vacation. Over the phone, she offered me the position of Program Director, which was part-time, all year long, the pay was good, and my kids would attend free. I said yes on the spot. She also asked that I bring in a copy of my bachelor's degree, as this job required it.

This daycare center was in the Arlington School District, as were my kids, which meant Sarah could take the school bus directly to my job. When I had planned to work as a substitute school teacher, I had searched thoroughly for a day-care program for David. Somehow, I hadn't found this one. Maybe that was because they were deliberately advertising as a summer camp to bring in more enrollees, but God was obviously working behind the scenes to get me this job.

I took my name off the substitute teachers lists and got most of my deposit back from the daycare facility where David was previously registered. I was overjoyed. As a Program Director, I'd be making more money than a substitute teacher, and I'd save on the cost of daycare since my kids would attend free. Also, I'd be working with kids, doing what I loved.

When I called to tell Andy, he was pleasantly surprised at such an arrangement. Then I began to realize why I hadn't gotten that other job I had so desperately wanted. Those other jobs paled by comparison. God had something much better. I learned that when God answers no or wait, it's for a good reason. Since I was prayerful and yielded to God at this time in my life, He was faithful to hold back any job that might have been good but not the best.

I really loved this job. God truly handpicked it for me. I'd never experienced any job involving so much responsibility. I worked from noon to six p.m. and was off on Tuesdays and weekends. The Director, Carol, and the other two Program Directors left by 1:00 p.m. After that, I ran the place. I was responsible for the safety and well-being of all seventy or so children ranging in ages from twelve weeks to twelve years.

As the one in charge, I oversaw the eight to ten teachers on duty during my shift, most of whom were college kids there on a temporary basis. A few regulars were older and were there for the duration. I was the go-to person for all first aid incidents. If there was a bloody nose, a scraped knee, bumped head, or even an asthma attack, the teacher/daycare worker would bring the child to me.

That summer, I began implementing the camp program for the older kids that the previous Program Director had already planned out. As the school year got underway, it was my primary responsibility to come up with recreation and craft ideas for the after-school kids, which is no easy task for that age group. I also organized a lot of fundraisers and was involved in the administrative front desk duties, such as collecting payments and dealing with parents' complaints. In such a child-oriented environment, I learned the essential skill of always maintaining a cheerful, upbeat attitude.

As parents began picking up their children at the end of the day, the student-to-teacher ratio dwindled. Since it wasn't feasible for Carol to pay anyone who didn't have to be there, and the state required only a certain number of staff for each age group, I was responsible to send teachers home each day when they were no longer needed.

Although this job was challenging, it was also rewarding and tons of fun. Since I love children, being with the kids was fun, but the job also required interacting with the parents, supervising a group of teachers, and resolving conflicts calmly and wisely. I was the problem solver for many of the issues that might arise. For example, I might have to keep a problem kid in my front office for acting up, talk to a parent when a problem warranted it, or listen to their complaints and quickly try to resolve their concerns.

The wonderful part of the job was having my kids there with me. David started out in the three-year-old room. I enjoyed taking David to work with me, and I was always around when he needed a hug. I was even able to put him down for a nap every day. Carol arranged for me to cover one of the teacher's thirty-minute lunch break in David's room. I was getting paid to snuggle my son until he fell asleep for his afternoon nap.

Part of my job was to receive the children off the bus to make sure all of them were accounted for. Needless to say, if a child on my list didn't get off the bus, that could be a problem. After school, Sarah took the bus to my job, where I was out by the front door to greet her. For the after-school kids, I organized kickball or whiffle ball games outside behind the building. Since Sarah was in that group, I spent time with her. In addition to craft projects and sports, we also used the kitchen to bake, we made lots of slime concoctions, and I organized inside games.

The young college kids who were teacher assistants (TAs) in the afterschool group had little ability or desire to motivate anyone or organize anything. They were more like babysitters who didn't feel they got paid enough to do more than just watch the kids. But I found it rewarding to interact with and encourage the kids, especially during the summer programs when we did a lot of other theme-related activities and had much more time together.

God used that job to grow and bless me and my children. I know I blessed many of the children there by giving them my time and genuinely caring about them. This job was very special to me, and I will always have fond memories of it.

After two years and two months working at this daycare center, I had to move on. Andy had been telling me for several months that he thought I should get back into County government. He felt that daycare was a dead-end job. As much as I loved the work, he was right. The job was perfect when my kids were very young while I transitioned back into the workforce, but it had no retirement plan, job security, or even paid sick time.

I began to take civil service exams for employment with Dutchess County, making a point to take all the exams available that I qualified for. I decided I would take the first job I was offered so I could get my foot in the door quickly. I could always take more exams later on, and with my BA, which I had received about a year before I resigned from Westchester County DSS, I would qualify for more positions.

It was a good thing I listened to my husband. The economy at this time in our area was declining. Many departments in

Dutchess County government weren't hiring. I interviewed for a Senior Office Assistant position with the Department of Mental Hygiene (DMH) at a continuing treatment center in Millbrook, New York. It didn't require a degree, but it seemed interesting and was the first and only interview that came up. After meeting with two interviewers a second time, I got the position. I was sure I'd love this job since I loved working with people and enjoyed clerical work.

Although this position paid more and I was able to accumulate benefit time and get back into the retirement system, this particular job at DMH became a dark experience for me. It plunged me into a four-year period of uncertainty, bitterness, deep depression, and diminishing faith.

Chapter 16

THE WILDERNESS YEARS

MY POSITION AT THE DUTCHESS COUNTY DEPARTMENT of Mental Hygiene (DMH) began on July 30, 2007, at their continuing treatment center (CTC) in Millbrook (MCTC), about a twenty-five-minute drive from home—a straight, beautiful drive on Route 82 through lush farmland, seemingly endless rolling hills, and breathtaking scenery. I enjoyed the drive to and from work and sometimes took that quiet opportunity to listen to sermons on The Bridge, a Christian radio station.

Unlike my position at the daycare center, I obviously couldn't bring my kids to work, so I had to find a good daycare arrangement. Sarah was nine and David, five. They didn't want to continue at the daycare center I'd just left since I was no longer working there.

By God's grace, I found a great arrangement right in my townhouse complex in Linda's home. This location was a blessing for Andy too since he got home from work by 4:30 p.m. and much preferred picking the kids up close to home. Linda only cared for a handful of children in addition to her own. Sarah and David became close friends with her children and looked forward to going there every day.

With my kids settled in at my neighbor's home daycare, I was eager to get back into County employment. I began with much joy and enthusiasm, but I became disheartened quickly. A group of employees at this office were cliquish. I replaced their beloved cohort who had just retired—ironically, another

Barbara. Apparently, we were similar in name only, and the group decided instantly that they didn't like me.

Unlike my previous job where the daycare workers were all accountable to me, here I was the low man on the totem pole. It had been nearly ten years since I'd worked in a clerical position while in Westchester County. I had forgotten about the hierarchal system that existed in County government, where every job had a grade level, and everyone tended to be treated accordingly.

Thanks to God in my life, I wasn't the same person I was ten years ago. I had earned my degree, gotten married, bought a house, was active in church, and was also the mother of two children. Now, I suddenly found myself immersed in a work environment where I felt neither respected nor accepted. For whatever reason, this little group of four chose not to like me. Their indifference and lack of communication with me was blatantly intentional. Unfortunately, I focused on the few that *didn't* like me, instead of the rest (about fourteen) who did.

That I was a Christian had come up in the first morning staff meeting while I was taking the minutes. One lady used a curse word while discussing a patient. She jokingly told me not to put that word in the minutes. I immediately responded that I wouldn't do that because I was a Christian. That comment upset one lady in particular, Julie.

For the duration of my four years working at MCTC, it was common knowledge that Julie hated me. Even Steve, the head of the unit and the other person she was also known to hate, told me on two separate occasions that she hated me. He and I talked together a lot, but although I never mentioned her name, he seemed to find it important to volunteer that information. Yet, it was apparent to everyone that she could barely tolerate him either, which was especially noticeable when he ran the numerous staff meetings. With exasperated sighs and rolling of the eyes, she was anything but discrete. If she didn't like someone, everyone knew it.

Hate is such a strong word. She didn't even know me, yet she hated me. If she simply didn't like me, that would have at least made sense, but I couldn't understand the hate. I really didn't care how she felt about me because it was clearly unjustified. I'd never done anything to her, so why should it bother me?

She seemed dissatisfied with life, much like I'd been, yet she had very likeable qualities. She was very intelligent and had a good sense of humor, but the way she treated me with such disdain for no reason whenever my job required that I communicate with her struck me as out-of-place. I wish I'd been in a better spiritual state back then and had been able to tell her about the Lord.

The patient population in this facility was classified as the "severely and persistently mentally ill," in other words, the most psychotic. Since most of the hospitals for mental illness had been shut down, they had no other place to go for treatment. They were bused in by vans for the day from their various group homes.

The treatment unit at MCTC consisted of a unit administrator, a psychiatric doctor, a nurse, a supervising recreation therapist, and about seven recreation therapy assistants (RTAs). The RTAs had a caseload of patients, conducted various groups, attended staff meetings, and counseled their patients individually as needed. What bothered me most during my four years working at MCTC was that the RTAs seemed, from what I observed, to act as if they were better than the clerical staff.

From the moment I walked in the door, I believed I was much more qualified and capable of doing their job than they were. I was convinced they had neither the training nor the qualifications to administer treatment to anyone. At the time, I thought of them as overly glorified and meagerly qualified. None of them (as far as I knew) had their bachelor's degree, yet I had a BA in Psychology and was doing secretarial work for them. The whole thing seemed unbearably unfair. Of course, I had no right to judge them or to feel angry. Probably most of them didn't lord it over me because of their job status, but that was how I felt at the time.

One aspect of the RTA's job was to write biweekly notes and treatment plans for the patients, due on certain dates in order to comply with the Office of Mental Health (OMH) requirements. Part of my job was to keep track of all the due dates on the treatment plans and remind the staff if they weren't done on time. Otherwise, the administrators at the main building in Poughkeepsie, who were overly fearful of not complying with OMH, would complain. The administrators also adhered, to an absurdly excessive degree in my opinion, to HIPPA laws of confidentiality.

Each day became more and more frustrating. Seeds of resentment caused deep roots of bitterness to grow in my heart that over time turned into an abiding, heavy weight of depression. I began to doubt God, and I blamed myself for somehow taking the wrong path and missing the job He had for me. I was convinced that I'd messed up and was stuck at the wrong job. After all, why would God allow me to get this job if it wasn't the right one for me? Why didn't He prevent me from getting it? I sank into a sea of confusion. All I knew was I just wanted a job where I could utilize my degree and live up to my potential.

Dragging myself to work every day with that gnawing discontentment about where I had to be forty hours a week became a laborious task. In my depression, I took refuge in the only thing I could think of. I began to binge on chocolate and junk food. Of course, I prayed about my situation, that I'd get a better job, which I vigorously pursued, but I wasn't finding any answers.

Clerically, my job at MCTC was easy—opening, closing, and transferring patient charts, typing monthly reports, making sure all the treatment plans were done on time, and maintaining OMH standards in my work, especially with patient charts. Clearly, God had gifted me with clerical skills. In the midst of a busy office, I always maintained an internal state of calm with regard to the work.

The other Senior Office Assistants in the other CTCs were sometimes stressed with the workload due to being understaffed, but I had downtime and frequently paid bills or googled in my office, when I had no work to do.

I supervised two part-time Office Assistants, and when I had one of them to cover the front office, I could hide away in my own spacious office with the door closed. I had that big office because I had to be where the patient charts were kept.

On several occasions when clerical staff in one of the other CTCs left for any extended amount of time, my staff would be pulled to cover those units for unspecified periods of time. For months, I was either down to one part-time Office Assistant or completely on my own. I never once complained, and that was only because when there was only one of us covering the front office, we were allowed to earn an hour comp time instead of taking a lunch hour. Seven hours of comp time translated into a day off.

My boss and her supervisor, who both worked at the main office in Poughkeepsie, were very happy with my work. They were especially appreciative of my willingness to give up my staff and work alone, and for my handling everything so smoothly and professionally. My supervisor's boss actually came down to my office to personally thank me for doing the job alone for so long a period of time. It was no hardship whatsoever. The work was easy, and I loved earning comp time.

Yes, the work was easy, but being in that office was hard. Since the day I started working there, I prayed fervently for a better job. My name was on a few other civil service jobs lists because when I took the exam for this job, I had taken the other ones I qualified for as well—Case Manager I and Social Welfare Worker I, both for the Department of Social Services. But nothing had materialized yet. It was always easier to get a County job at lower level positions.

Every day I continued to search the job postings on the County website at work. I took each and every civil service exam that came up for positions that required a degree and that would get me out of there and into a new and rewarding career.

I didn't want to waste my qualifications on any clerical jobs like the one I currently had.

Finally, I got an interview for a Youth Worker position with the Youth Bureau that paid about $10,000 more per year. Extremely excited about the prospect of this job, I felt good as I eagerly anticipated this interview, and my depression lifted. I was convinced that God had this job in mind for me. Why else would He allow me to go on an interview for a job that I really wanted if He wasn't planning to give it to me?

After working at a daycare center and teaching Sunday school at church, I knew I loved working with children and was good at it. The Youth Bureau sounded like the perfect department for me.

The interview lasted almost an hour. The lady asked a lot of questions. I felt it went very well. I was told that it would be a two-month wait until all the interviews were done and the decision was made.

Several months went by, and I heard nothing. But I knew they couldn't have made a decision yet because I hadn't received a sorry-we-didn't-choose-you letter. The wait was unnerving, but I was leery of calling and sounding like a pest. After waiting another month or two, I finally called.

No one had gotten the job. The position had been closed for budgetary reasons. The economy was bad at this time. In fact, I had actually landed my current job immediately before a county-wide freeze had begun, which remained in effect for the next few years in most departments. I was actually extremely lucky to have gotten in. Had I waited any longer, I probably wouldn't have gotten a County job at all.

By all rights, I should have been thankful for my present job. God obviously gifted me to manage the clerical work of the unit smoothly and stress-free while also raising two children. Taking care of a house—endless laundry, dishes, paying bills, not to mention running the kids around and helping with homework every night—provided more than enough stress for me to handle. I should have been thankful to have an easy, low-stress job at this time in my life.

This job, in fact, provided a precious opportunity for me to be with David as he started school and was away from me for the first time. When I started at the Millbrook CTC, we were told that the building would be undergoing renovations, and that we'd have to be relocated for what turned out to be a year.

We were temporarily located in an office building in Lagrange, New York, three minutes driving distance from my son's elementary school. On many of my lunch hours, I was able to volunteer in David's Kindergarten class. What an enormous blessing it was to be there for David as he transitioned into his first year of public school.

I also interviewed for Case Manager with Child Protective Services, a unit within the Department of Social Services. This position was also an increase in salary, involved working with children, and required a degree. Despite the job freeze, Social Services was always a busy department with high turnover. When I didn't get that job either, I really couldn't understand why God was putting me on such an emotional rollercoaster. I'd get my hopes up and feel good, only to be let down again.

As my daily routine dragged on, my contempt for MCTC worsened. My whole demeanor became antagonistic. Unlike those other jobs on the unit that involved helping others, I felt my job was just meaningless paperwork. It felt intensely unfair.

I did a lot of soul searching during this time. I was perplexed at how I could have wound up at this job where my potential was wasted. I knew I could continue to take exams and eventually something better would turn up, but that didn't seem good enough.

Deep down in my heart I knew I should be thankful I had a job when there were hardly any job openings in the County.

I needed to get rid of my consuming negativity, but that didn't seem possible.

At last, my chance to break out into a new line of work came. One of the lists I'd been on for a while was Social Welfare Worker (SWW). They finally got down to my name on the list, and that canvass letter came. With numerous opportunities for training and advancement, Social Services is a great department to work for. The interview went well, and I got the job. I was elated. I was getting out of MCTC and starting a new career.

When I had worked at Social Services years back in Westchester County, the equivalent for SWW there was Eligibility Examiner. Getting this particular job had been my career aspiration for all those years I was working there, but I didn't have the necessary degree at that time. My time had finally come.

After four years at MCTC, I left joyfully to start at the Department of Social Services as a Social Welfare Worker in the Temporary Assistance Intake Unit. I was determined to learn everything I could, to work my hardest, and to do my job well. No way was I *not* going to succeed. I put my all into this job. But despite my high expectations and tireless efforts, after seven months, I was fired.

I really believed this job in Social Services was precisely what I needed to launch my career. I knew I wouldn't fail. But I did. Although I had no idea at the time, God had other plans for me. Despite what I thought I wanted, He was still working behind the scenes helping me get to the right place. Later on, I realized I didn't really know what I wanted or what was best for me. I thought I did, but my own self-serving aspirations misguided me.

My motives were all wrong. I didn't really want to help people. I wanted to be in the helping field because it made me look good, and I'd feel better about myself. Just like working at MCTC made me feel bad about myself and unhappy because I thought clerical work was menial, I believed moving up to a higher position would make me feel good about myself, and I'd be happy.

While I didn't realize it at the time, my self-esteem was inextricably tied to my job. I had no idea what was to come in my near future and how God would radically change me.

Chapter 17

Shattered Dreams

My first two to three months as a Social Welfare Worker were primarily a training period. I sat in on client interviews and made a point of taking copious notes, as I was determined to learn everything. Foremost in my mind was the conviction that I would do well and eventually move up in the ranks.

To sum up briefly, this job entailed determining eligibility for the people who came into the Temporary Assistance (TA) office to apply for various services. All of the applicant's possible sources of income had to be determined before they would be considered for benefits. Temporary assistance was supposed to be a last resort.

The other main contingency to receiving benefits was that applicants had to be pursuing employment in measurable amounts of interviews per week. If they were suffering from addiction or mental illness, they could be exempted from that requirement.

The TA Intake Unit was well-known as the worst unit to work in, and employee turnover was high. After the Reception Unit, TA Intake was the frontlines of Social Services. The influx of people seemed endless. Coming in right off the streets, the people were obviously in dire situations.

The TA workers' caseloads were enormous. At any given time of day, the front reception area was always packed. That reality alone speaks volumes about the struggles too many people face with the basic needs of life. Bottom line, the most difficult part of the job, and perhaps the main reason workers want out, is the stress of trying to keep up with the large caseloads.

I got along well with nearly everyone except Fran. As the supervisor of the TA Intake Unit, she was a no-nonsense, brusque person. I decided immediately that I didn't like her. I started off badly by being judgmental of her, and she returned the same sentiments toward me. Later on, I realized she was actually a nice person and compassionate toward the client population she served.

During my downtime, I read as much information as I could. I was getting a good grasp on what I needed to do and was beginning to understand how all the pieces fit together. Some of the workers there thought I was doing fine, and the truth was that I had been doing reasonably well.

Admittedly, the main thing that slowed me down was the computer codes used to enter client information. With so many codes, we actually had a tabbed book to contain them all. Also, waiting for other units to do their part in the process or waiting for other paperwork slowed me down in completing my work.

Fran didn't like that I bothered other workers when I had a question as to how to proceed with my work. I didn't really have a choice. I had to get my work done, as it was piling up.

After about six months, she came into my office with terminations papers for me to sign. I had a feeling it was forthcoming. She had written me up on two previous occasions for stating that I could help two different clients when in fact they were not eligible for services. She was right about that. I was at fault, but I didn't think that warranted firing me.

Interestingly, before I actually saw what Fran had brought in for me to sign, I found myself inwardly hoping and praying that it *was* termination papers. To my surprise, when I realized I was officially fired, I immediately felt a surge of happiness and a great sense of relief.

I thought the end of my career would be devastating, but I just wanted to get out of there and away from the enormous stress of my case records piling up and scrambling around trying to process them. Being so focused on succeeding, I hadn't been aware of how much I hated the work.

I was never going to quit, though. All along, I believed I would get through the initial difficulties, and things would get better. I kept a positive attitude as I plodded through my work, ever hopeful that I was going to get organized and eventually manage my work smoothly. I hadn't realized how much I dreaded going to work.

The thing that caused such anxiety and stress, beginning as I drove to work each morning, were the piles of cases awaiting me that continued to grow. It was frustrating not to be able to move so many files out of my office because I was waiting for a client's paperwork, for more information from another unit, or for some other particular detail.

Regardless of all the stress, I was determined to work through it. I was convinced that after putting a year or two under my belt, I would be caught up and things would run like clockwork. After all, I'd excelled at every single thing I'd prayerfully endeavored to do since becoming a new person in Christ. I was convinced God would help me succeed at this as well.

Yet, for reasons I would fully understand later, He allowed me to fail. Ultimately, God is in control of everything regardless of what we might will to achieve. Ironically, what seemed like a devastating event, God used for my good. Far more important, unseen eternal things were going on, it turned out, than for me to succeed at this job.

I gladly signed the paperwork and finished my two weeks with joy. My reaction and behavior didn't go unnoticed by at least one of the young workers who had started with me. She commented to me that I showed unique character under the circumstances because I was still working hard and didn't seem to be bitter or hold a grudge.

As soon as I was fired, I called my previous supervisor, Lynn, at the Department of Mental Hygiene (DMH). I guess it really *does* make a difference whether or not you burn your bridges behind you. In this case, my bridges were intact. I had a four-year history of clerically running one of the continuing treatment sites, and they knew me as a reliable and competent employee.

Lynn wanted to take me back, but MCTC no longer existed. She did, however, have a position for me at the main DMH building in Poughkeepsie. God was working in my favor. Lynn had a specific reason for wanting me back.

During the four years I'd been working at MCTC, there had been talk about the CTCs (Continuing Treatment Centers) being privatized due to the enormous cost to the County to run those programs. Contracting out to another company was a lot more cost effective. It was also rumored that many of the other County-run treatment facilities would be closed later.

Knowing the ultimate future of MCTC, everyone was eager to jump ship to their advantage rather than remain on a sinking one. Of course, I wanted to get out for other reasons.

About six months or so before I had received my promotion, the anticipated shutdown was already in the works. After a period of bidding for the continuing treatment centers, a private company was chosen and entered into a contractional agreement with the County.

All the CTC employees were catapulted into a state of panic and confusion. Many were able to take early retirement packages. Depending on seniority, the rest were tossed around to other sites. People wound up working in places they had never expected but were thankful to still have jobs.

Having been at Dutchess County only four years, I would probably have been bumped out of a job. But by God's grace, I got out at the perfect time when I took that promotion to Social Services. Now, even though all the CTCs were no longer county-run, I was fortunate to get back into the same department I'd left, the Department of Mental Hygiene (DMH).

I lost no continuity in full-time employment. I left Social Services on a Friday and drove right over to DMH that Monday, which was also in Poughkeepsie, about ten minutes away from my previous job.

I started back at DMH in Poughkeepsie in February of 2012. My supervisor, Lynn, was a Support Services Manager, and was directly accountable to the Commissioner, Dr. Glatt.

The first floor of the Main DMH building housed Reception, the Hudson Valley Mental Health Clinic, a cafeteria, and several other mental and health programs for the developmentally and physically disabled. My office was on the second (top) floor, just down the hall from Lynn. Everyone I worked with and all of the clerical and reception staff on the first floor were extremely pleasant. I knew many of them from prior phone contact or from seeing them in passing when I had attended meetings at this building a few times each year.

Starting a new job where I already had a familiarity with many friendly people was great. Unlike the remote, off-site location out in the country where I worked for four years, the main DMH building was large and spread out, full of activity with the hustle and bustle of all the programs going on.

The timing of my termination was perfect for Lynn. She needed me to go back to the previous MCTC unit to pack up patient charts, files, as well as other clerical drawers and storage rooms. Everything remaining in our clerical cabinets had to be logged, packed, and labeled, and that wasn't going to be done by the new corporation's staff. As busy as Lynn was, she didn't have time, nor did she want to do that job. Who better to do it than me since I knew the unit?

This time, going to MCTC wasn't depressing. Even though I was back there because I had failed at DSS, being back in my bright, sunny office, packing up and closing down our presence there felt like a fresh start. I also trained the new corporation's clerical staff on various forms and procedures. Even the new Unit Administrator had numerous clerical questions for me.

When all of that was done, I returned to DMH in Poughkeepsie. The atmosphere was professional and friendly. I loved coming to work. I enjoyed the work and the people. Routine responsibilities kept me minimally occupied. Often, though, like at MCTC, I had nothing to do until Lynn gave me a project. Then I'd be busy for a while.

At DMH, unrest began to elevate again as concrete plans were in place to close at least two more county-run mental health sites in the very near future. My job stability, once again, became tenuous. When Lynn, who handled personnel in the department, calculated everyone's seniority in the clerical job lines, she told me that I would most likely wind up losing my job with these shut downs.

She strongly recommended that I put my name on the Preferred Eligibility List for my title, Senior Office Assistant. This would guarantee me a job that came up in my title in another county department. Although I wanted to stay where I was, I knew it was too risky.

As it turned out, my name was first on the list. I simply had to wait for the next available opening. Unlike other jobs where I would have to go for an interview, I was guaranteed the job.

Having been so busy in general, and then with all the bouncing around from DMH to DSS and back to DMH, I had neglected to get my annual mammogram for two-and-a-half years. When my husband discovered a lump in my left breast, I decided I'd better get in, albeit late, for a mammogram and an ultrasound.

Never could I have imagined the horrific road two routine procedures would force me to travel.

Part V
The Dreaded Disease

Chapter 18

A Sudden Diagnosis

After accepting the Lord into my heart seventeen years prior to this time, God had blessed me with great health, spiritual growth, and, despite some struggles, a truly great life, as well as keeping my family heathy and safe from harm. Although my husband has a few physical issues, thank God, he doesn't have any life-threatening disease, and is still able to function in spite of arthritic pain and other non-life-threatening ailments.

I was the healthy one in our marriage. I'd never been seriously ill a day in my life, and I always had, what seemed to Andy, unending energy. Due to his physical limitations, I was always the one outside playing ball with the kids, biking, swimming, or taking them to playgrounds and parties.

As I played outside with the kids, Andy cooked, calling us in when dinner was ready. I had the life. Another blessing years in advance, God enabled me to be coordinated in sports so I could play ball with the kids, since physically, Andy couldn't.

My physical health, boundless energy, and skill with sports were a major source of joy and self-confidence. I was the only mom in our townhouse community who actually played with her kids as well as with the other neighborhood children. I was the cool mom, and my kids appreciated it.

But I had become too comfortable with my blessed, easy life. My spiritual walk began to decline. Totally unaware it was happening, I became a complacent Christian, lukewarm, content to remain spiritually stagnant and not grow any closer to God.

Throughout my new life of blessing, I still struggled with bouts of depression, but I regularly swept those feelings under the notorious rug, hiding this secret from others, and even from myself. Since I wasn't fully connected to God, the true and only source of satisfaction, it's not surprising my joy had diminished. I was much like the Israelites who always seemed to turn away from God when things got good.

My turning away wasn't an outright denial or an intentional departure from God. It was a gradual slipping away from growing in my relationship with Him. All those years being miserable at MCTC, feeling overwhelmed with housework and kids, my focus was on myself instead of on God. Unknowingly, I'd pushed Him out, cutting off my source of power and joy, and my spiritual walk paid the price. I no longer had a closeness with Him.

I still went to church on Sundays, and I always committed one night a week to a home Bible study group, but beyond that, I was as close to God as I was capable of getting without His mighty hand of intervention. Somehow, I deceived myself into thinking I was truly a good Christian and had a great relationship with God, but I wasn't really abiding in Him daily or surrendering my life to Him, or even pursuing a closer relationship with Him.

Just as the Israelites needed to be brought back to God, often by harsh means, I needed something to jar me awake, change my course, and cause me to experience a deep closeness with Him. God used famine, war, and captivity to get the Israelites' attention. He got my attention with a sudden diagnosis that I thought could never happen to me.

My life had been redeemed, and I was blessed in many ways, but God wanted so much more for me. He wanted to bring me into a profound closeness with Him and show me more of Himself. He wanted to change me to be more like His Son by helping me to love others the way He does. He says in

His Word, "For whom He foreknew, He also predestined to be conformed to the image of His Son, that He might be the first-born among many brethren" (Romans 8:29). I needed a serious makeover spiritually if I was to fulfill His plan for my life.

In my pride, I truly believed my relationship with God was good. But the fact that I had no joy in my life should have been a red flag that I was shutting Him out. Thank God, He intervened, or I would have continued on the same path.

In the throes of depleted contentment, I escaped into the quick and easy fix with the only addiction I knew and loved—food, particularly the sweet variety. Although most of the time I tried to eat healthfully, I had an ongoing problem with sugar. Even when things were going well, that craving often reared its ugly head, but even more so when I was in the midst of my persistent depression. My binges became a regular occurrence.

Whenever I indulged, as I did at least three times a week, I felt guilty. I worried about getting diabetes. I knew I was playing with fire and pushing my luck. I also knew I couldn't splurge on sweets and junk food and expect no adverse effects in my body. I feared if I didn't get control of it soon, I could wind up with a horrible disease, possibly even cancer.

Consequences of some kind had to be looming around the corner as I continued to wreak havoc on my body. I kept reassuring myself that I would soon get it under control, but that never happened. Instead, I continued this pattern for several years, during which time I gained about thirty pounds.

Since I'd always been healthy, getting cancer seemed remote. Yet, I still worried about it when I binged. Then I'd immediately reason that God would never allow cancer into my life, not after all I'd been through. God is not evil or sadistic, so I easily concluded that after I had overcome so much emotional trauma from my childhood and teen years, surely He wouldn't plague me now with a serious physical disease. That just didn't seem fair. I was sure a merciful God wouldn't do that. I later came to realize that God is beyond figuring out, and He often allows the unexpected. Yet, He knows exactly what He is doing.

Every year when I had my mammogram, I was told I was fine, totally clean. The lumps and pain I felt were just cysts. I had fibrocystic breast disease, which is common in many women. I thought the lump Andy had found was nothing but the usual cyst, but I made the appointment anyway.

I went to the Dutchess Radiology Associates (DRA), where I'd always gone for my routine mammograms. They performed a mammogram as well as an ultrasound. As is customary for DRA, they gave me their preliminary findings right away.

After the radiologist looked at the results, I was called back into the ultrasound room where he and the technician who had just conducted the ultrasound were waiting. With a somber expression I was not expecting, this soft-spoken man told me with apparent concern that my pictures look "very suspicious."

He explained that I had a tumor mass that may or may not be malignant but that, in either case, it would have to be surgically removed. As he told me this news, I felt something odd going on inside me.

"How suspicious?" I asked. "What are the odds this is actually cancer?"

My questions most likely appeared to convey fear and worry, but as he patiently answered, I felt an almost unrecognizable, vague excitement within me at the news that I might actually have cancer. On some very ambiguous, barely conscious level, I hoped I did.

My life felt mundane, stagnant—working nine to five, tending to my kids' needs, and cleaning my house repeatedly. I had already concluded years ago that apart from a relationship with God, I could have no real, lasting joy, but I wasn't there anymore, and I didn't seem to know how to get back there. I was prone to depression and eating binges, with cycles of guilt and new diets I could never stick with. Yet, I hadn't found the root cause of my emptiness—that I needed more of God in my life.

The radiologist recommended I get two biopsies, both a mammogram-guided and an ultrasound-guided biopsy. Since he was not my doctor, he said he couldn't make the appointment or arrange for those procedures. I needed to contact my gynecologist right away. I gave him his name and asked if he'd contact him, and he agreed to call that day.

I still wasn't overly alarmed. They'd called me back in for a repeat picture on many occasions because of the difficulty in reading the image due to my dense tissue. Everything had always turned out fine. But this wasn't a repeat picture to get a better look. They actually wanted two biopsies. I'd never thought I would ever need a biopsy on any part of my body.

That evening after the kids were in bed and Andy and I were comfortably settled in, I finally told him. I wasn't feeling worried about it, as I assumed I only had cysts. I thought Andy would feel the same way, but he began to console me with deep compassion, which caught me off guard and seemed almost eerie.

My gynecologist, who'd spoken with the radiologist, called me the next day to tell me he had set up the biopsies and gave me the details. He also told me that I should see a breast surgeon and gave me the name and number of Dr. Z at the Dyson Center for Cancer Care.

The next day during my lunch hour, as though I was simply running another errand, I arrived at the Dyson Center, which is next to Vassar Brothers Hospital in Poughkeepsie, not too far from my place of work at DMH. As I got out of my car and stood in the parking lot in front of that massive building with its large letters, Dyson Center for Cancer Care, staring me in the face, an ominous thought began to emerge. Was this building and what it represents to be a new part of my life? Was I a cancer patient now?

But all I had was a routine mammogram and ultrasound. Nothing was conclusive at this point. Why should I be here at this place? After all, I hadn't even had the biopsies yet. How could anybody possibly know anything or even dare to suspect anything without the definitive biopsy results?

Shortly after arriving and finding my way into the waiting room on the second floor of this huge place, I was called into one of the examining rooms. A really friendly, cheerful nurse asked me a series of routine questions. To my confusion and vague disbelief, she kept using the word, *boobs,* when referring to the area in question. That seemed a little unprofessional and a bit too informal. Maybe she was trying to put me at ease.

When she left the room, a nurse practitioner came in and introduced herself as Tammy. She was very pleasant and asked me how I was feeling and then immediately got to the point. With straightforward determination, she told me that I had cancer. Then, she gave me a hug and told me, with what seemed to be genuine compassion, that she was here for me and would help me in any way possible.

In awkward silence, she stood there quietly for a moment waiting for me to react or say something or break down and cry. I can be an emotional person, but I definitely lean more toward the logical side. I didn't say anything except, "Really?"

I imagine Tammy must have been the go-to person to break the news to new cancer patients. I assumed she was the one with the "skills" to calm hysterical women and give them the hope and encouragement they needed in the face of such sudden, horrific news. That can't be an easy job. She seemed to have the knowledge to answer questions and the compassion to be reassuring that everything was going to be okay and that they were going to do everything possible.

The reason she wanted to see me now, before the biopsies, was to examine me before any possible swelling or bruising occurred as a result of the biopsy procedures which could alter the appearance of my tumor. She also wanted an MRI done prior to the biopsies to see if there was more cancer in my left breast that might have been missed by the mammogram and ultrasound.

Finally, I asked, "How can you possibly make this diagnosis without a biopsy?" It seemed unprofessional.

Tammy then proceeded to show me my pictures. Confidently and patiently, she went on to explain that she'd seen this many times before. The large tumor on the ultrasound picture was solid, not a cyst. The size and shape of it indicated it was cancerous. The mammogram showed many microcalcifications along the medial section which clearly appeared to be in the process of forming another mass.

I then asked, "Couldn't you be wrong?"

"Yes," she admitted, "I could be wrong. It has happened before."

I didn't know what to believe. In parting, I said, "I'm not really convinced until I see the biopsy results."

I already had the mammogram and ultrasound biopsies scheduled. And now, following this visit at Dyson, I also had an MRI scheduled.

My lunch hour almost over, I drove back to work, pondering this new revelation. Did I actually have cancer? I had to admit I was beginning to believe I probably did. I know this must sound strange, but I suddenly felt privileged.

I knew God didn't give me this cancer or cause it to happen because His Word clearly says only good comes from Him. "Every good gift and every perfect gift is from above, and comes down from the Father of lights, with whom there is no variation or shadow of turning" (James 1:17).

Every tragedy we experience comes from this sin-stricken, diseased world, not from God. I also believe that God will never allow a tragedy into someone's life unless He plans to use it for good.

God in His infinite power, of course, could have prevented this. He chose not to, though, and I was sure it was because He had a better plan. I began to realize that God had a plan and purpose in mind to use this tragedy for good. I just didn't know exactly what, but I knew it was for something good.

In the car that day, I truly believed He was going to bless me through this experience. I was convinced He was going to use this disease to mold me into the person He wanted me to be, and that excited me.

Driving back to work, I felt peace and even joy because I knew God was with me and was going to use me for His glory and His purpose. No wonder I felt privileged.

Romans 8:28 immediately came into my mind. "And we know that all things work together for good to those who love God, to those who are the called according to His purpose." No matter what hardship befalls a child of God, He will always turn it around and use it for our good, which is to make us more like Christ.

Romans 8:28 promises something good, and Romans 8:29 explains what that good is. "For whom He foreknew, He also predestined to be conformed to the image of His Son, that He might be the firstborn among many brethren." The good is being conformed to the image of His Son, which means to be surrendered to His will as Jesus was, and to learn to love like He loves, and to accomplish the things He has planned for us.

Understandably, Romans 8:28 is a popular verse with Christians who are going through difficult times. But this verse had meant a lot to me even before this diagnosis. God had used my childhood adversities for good in that I easily discovered the void in my heart and became more desperate in my search for answers. I thank God for my horrible past! It led me to Him. Had I not gone through that childhood ordeal, I might have never found God.

I believe God wastes nothing we go through but uses it for His purpose, His glory, and always for our best and to bless others. He can turn anything around for good, for "...with God all things are possible" (Mark 10:27).

In the Gospel of John, Jesus is asked by His disciples why a particular man was born blind. They asked Jesus if it was because of sin in this man's life or because his parents had sinned. Jesus replied that it was neither, but that he was born blind so that the work of God would be revealed through his life (John 9:1-3).

Jesus went on to heal this man of his blindness. This man then became a visible, living testimony to the love and power of God to all those people with whom he came into contact. No doubt, many others came to an acceptance of God, through Jesus His Son, also wanting that same love and power that had miraculously changed this man, who proclaimed, "...One thing I know: that though I was blind, now I see" (John 9:25).

Although God doesn't bring blindness or cancer into our lives, He uses these tragedies to work His healing power in us, both physically and spiritually. When others witness the change God's power and love has produced in our lives, they will want to give their lives over to Him, to be with Him forever.

That hour off for lunch felt like I'd been gone a month. I was thankful my biopsies were coming up soon. Although I dreaded them, I would finally have a definitive answer.

Chapter 19

God Never Allows More Than We Can Handle

SHORTLY AFTER MY NAME WAS PUT ON THE PREFERRED eligible list for Senior Office Assistant, a canvass letter came in the mail. Of all places, this position was in the Department of Social Services (DSS), where I'd left only about five months prior.

I had an interview with Maureen, who would be my supervisor if I chose to take the job. She knew the job was already mine if I wanted it, but she wanted to tell me what the position entailed. I would be working with computer templates producing various summonses from the Family Court petitions I was given and typing other various court documents.

This position was on the second floor in the Child Support Enforcement Unit (CSEU). My previous position at DSS had been on the first floor. Located at 60 Market Street in Poughkeepsie, DSS took up the entire building with four floors of various services. About three-hundred and fifty employees worked in DSS, and thirty-six in the CSEU unit.

Although I liked working at DMH, many people were leaving, and I had no choice but to jump ship too. With imminent closures on the horizon, I had to anchor into another position quickly, lest I lose my job at DMH and be out of the County altogether. I said yes to the job and was told I'd hear about a start date within a few days.

Next on the docket were the biopsies I so feared. Simply anticipating the unknown, I was panic-stricken. I'd never experienced surgery or any serious medical procedure. The thought of two invasive biopsies involving needles and tissue, as well as pain, terrified me. Such things happened to other people, not to me. I'd always been convinced that I would never have to go through such a horrible procedure.

The day finally arrived. Andy came with me and, as we made our way into the reception area of DRA Imaging, my fear of the unknown grew beyond comprehension. They were going to do both the mammogram-guided and the ultrasound-guided biopsies that morning. It was definitely better to get them both over with at once. I felt enough anxiety with *one* visit.

By the time they called me in, I was beside myself with panic. This wasn't supposed to happen to me, I continued to remind myself. I wondered how in the world they were going to do these procedures. It wasn't like going to the dentist where, although it was painful and unpleasant, at least I knew the drill. Here, the anticipation of the unknown was unbearable.

One of the technicians, sensing my obvious apprehension, immediately put herself into caring mode. Poor woman! She might have thought this would be an easy morning for her, but I was her first patient that day. But she certainly rose to the occasion. Reassuringly, she talked me through every detail as they laid me down on my side and explained that they had to find the area and then remove six strands of tissue.

As the nurses and technicians continued to describe each step, I lay there with my eyes closed until the procedure was over. It was tedious work, but I remained motionless. After about half an hour, it was finally over. I was actually surprised that it didn't really hurt much at all.

I'd gotten through it! After days of worry, what an enormous relief to finally be done with it. Despite my terror, it actually turned out not that bad.

I still had to go into the ultrasound room for the second biopsy. A friend at work, Martha, told me she had one of these biopsies and that the needle made a disgusting sound as it circled around pulling tissue samples. As I walked in, I wondered why she had shared that with me.

They had me lie down, this time on my back, as they explained that they had to first find the area via the ultrasound procedure. Then I was given a shot of Novocain, and they described how they were going to put a cylinder-shaped object on the area and that it would pull out samples. I had never watched whenever I had blood drawn, I certainly wasn't going to look at whatever was going on in that room.

The ultrasound biopsy wasn't that bad either, but it did make a disgusting sound. It wasn't fun but definitely not painful and went much faster than the previous biopsy. Thank the Lord! I can be such a scaredy-cat sometimes, but many people were praying for me.

I went back to the waiting room to meet up with Andy. Although thankful the dreaded biopsies were finally over, I couldn't help but wonder if these two tests weren't just the beginning of many more such procedures to come. After knowing nothing but good health my whole life, I wondered if this was to be my new way of life.

I was scheduled to see Dr. Z at the Dyson Center about five days after the biopsies so he could go over the findings with me. Tammy, the nurse practitioner, called me at home the night before I was to go in for that appointment. The biopsy results had come in a little early. I took the phone into the guest bathroom so the kids wouldn't hear.

Tammy told me the biopsies confirmed I had cancer. Based on the previous office visit with her, that didn't come as much of a shock.

"The kind that requires chemo?" I asked.

"Yes," she said.

"The kind of chemo where you lose your hair?"

Again, she answered in the affirmative.

Once again, she seemed to be waiting for a reaction from me, so I said, "It's a win/win situation any way you look at it. If I live, that's a definite win, but if I die, that's even better because I'll be in heaven."

That was the only logical yet true thing I could think to say. God knew what He was doing. Having said that, though, I still had a strong yearning to live. I wanted more time with Andy, the joyful experience of watching my kids grow up, make their way in the world, and give me grandchildren, and to do the work I knew God planned for me. I didn't know the details yet, but I knew He had incredible plans for my life because His Word is clear and His promises are always faithful: "For I know the thoughts that I think toward you, says the LORD, thoughts of peace and not of evil, to give you a future and a hope" (Jeremiah 29:11).

After my phone call with Tammy, I told Andy. I began to realize that this news was too much to wrap my brain around all at once. I had to take it in stride, one new development at a time. Romans 8:28 never left my mind. Without that verse, nothing in this situation made any sense, and I would have fallen apart at the seams. But that verse gave me peace, sustaining hope, and even joy in the midst of what was to become a horrendous ordeal.

As long as I held on to Romans 8:28, I had reason for joy because that verse held all the promise and reassurance I needed. Even while the physical trials became long and trying, that verse provided a glimmer of hope that there was light at the end of this arduous tunnel, and eventually something good on the horizon.

Again, on my lunch hour, I left for the Dyson Center, about a ten-minute drive away. Only this time I wasn't going to have to deal with any news alone. Andy was meeting me there. In the office with us was Dr. Z, Tammy, and a nurse to discuss the biopsy results and surgical options.

I was diagnosed with three types of breast cancer—triple positive. My cancer was estrogen/progesterone receptor positive and human epidermal growth factor receptor 2 positive (HER2+). They couldn't believe I'd never taken an estrogen-containing drug as some women do for difficult menopausal symptoms.

To them, I looked fit, energetic, and healthy, but there I was with all this cancer in my left breast. Until that time, I hadn't *known* I had a large, invasive, cancerous tumor in my breast, so it was easy to run around and play sports with my kids as though nothing was wrong.

Dr. Z told me that the tumor was large enough to put me at Stage II. The tumor mass, he said, was invasive ductal carcinoma. It had originated from the duct but had invaded tissue outside the duct.

The other area they found along the medial section of my breast was ductal carcinoma in situ (DCIS). It was still confined to the duct. Both areas had originated in the ducts as opposed to from the lobes (lobular).

At this time, I was also told that the MRI showed something suspicious in the back of my left breast. Now I would need an MRI-guided biopsy of that area, which would be biopsy number three.

Dr. Z was one of the calmest and gentlest doctors I have ever met, which made him easy to talk with. He explained all of the surgical options. If I wanted breast preservation, I could go with a lumpectomy, but radiation would be necessary in addition to chemotherapy. Of course, that was only if the MRI biopsy showed nothing. If the MRI biopsy showed more cancer, then the lumpectomy was out. I would need a mastectomy.

He further clarified that if I definitely chose the mastectomy, the MRI biopsy wouldn't be necessary since he'd be removing everything anyway. But if I wanted to go with the lumpectomy, the MRI biopsy would be required to ensure there was no cancer in the posterior section of my breast.

I actually saw a way out of getting the MRI biopsy, but I would have to commit to a mastectomy. I just wasn't sure, but I decided I needed to know if I had more cancer, or if I even had the option of a lumpectomy before I made a decision about surgery, so we scheduled the MRI biopsy.

Now that the surgical discussion had been dealt with, Dr. Z and Tammy were anxious to get me over to see an oncologist since the HER2+ part of my cancer was extremely aggressive. I would have to receive chemo before surgery. They called the Hudson Valley Cancer Center, a place I would soon become very familiar with, and sent me to see Dr. S., who would be expecting me, since they were faxing over my paperwork.

The oncology clinic, although its own entity, was in the St. Frances Hospital complex. Getting over there from Dyson was a ten-minute drive. I called my job from Dyson to let them know I'd be out for the rest of the afternoon.

When we arrived at the HV Cancer Center, throngs of people filled the waiting room, most of them sick with some form of cancer or blood disorder, waiting to get their chemo or blood treatment. It was an entirely different world than I'd ever before had to deal with.

Now I was part of it. I just couldn't believe I was a cancer patient. I wasn't even sure what chemo really was or how a person actually received it in the *Infusion* Room. The word sounded creepy. It conjured up images of lying in a machine completely vulnerable while someone poured poison into all the veins of my body. Couldn't they just call the infusion room the *healing* room?

After a thirty-minute wait, we were finally called in to see Dr. S. She was very energetic, cheerful, and personable, as well as young and pregnant. She swept into the room like a whirlwind of information, speaking way too quickly and almost making my head spin. She assumed way too much about my knowledge of cancer and its treatments.

She was extremely kind and took the time to explain everything to me, but by the time she was finished, I had more questions than answers, none of which I could have articulated that day. How could I possibly grasp all this new information?

The estrogen part of the cancer made sense. Basically, I somehow had too much estrogen for my body to handle. Estrogens were in foods and in the environment, some kinds were good; others, very detrimental. I was lucky, though, she told me. If I was going to have cancer, this was the best kind to have because it was treatable with chemo. I just couldn't fit the word lucky into the picture.

The HER2+ part of my cancer was different. They had no idea how that originated. But thank God, a new drug, Herceptin, was recently approved that had been proven to be effective in treating HER2+ because this type of breast cancer is extremely aggressive. If I were to have gotten this HER2+ type of cancer years earlier, before the approval of Herceptin, I would have died within a relatively short period of time. The only problem with Herceptin was that it not only attacked the cancer cells but also the heart. It had the potential to cause reduced heart function and congestive heart failure.

Dr. S continued to explain that in addition to Herceptin, I would need the chemo drugs Carboplatin and Taxotere to treat the estrogen/progesterone part of my cancer. These particular chemo drugs were very strong and carried their own array of side effects that most people know about, even if they've never had cancer. These include losing hair, throwing up, lowered immune system, and lethargy. Being on these three drugs was called TCH therapy.

She put me on a chemo schedule of Taxotere and Carboplatin infusions every third Monday for what she referred to as six cycles which would last for about four-and-a-half months. I was to receive my Herceptin infusions on Mondays, every week. After this regimen, I would have my surgery.

After surgery, Herceptin would only be given once a month for about nine more months, for a little over a year in total. If that weren't enough, the day after each chemo treatment, I had to go back to the infusion room to get a shot of Neulasta to boost my immune system after the onslaught of the two chemo drugs.

My life drastically changed. I was catapulted into a barrage of tests, procedures, medications, blood work regularly...and six cycles of chemo. Dr. S took out her prescription pad and began to write with incredible speed, as she briefly discussed each one of the meds and procedures I would need in order to get started with treatment. By the time she was done, she had handed me about eight prescription sheets. I held them in my hand, dumbfounded, my jaw agape.

To be cleared to start chemo, I needed an echocardiogram to make sure my heart was strong enough to handle the Herceptin. Because Taxotere could damage my veins, I also required a surgical procedure to internally lodge a port into my chest, which connected to a vein, in order to receive my infusions. Once I had the port, all the drugs would go in through it.

This large, steel structure protruded visibly, like a large lump, from underneath my skin on the right side of my chest. I couldn't help but touch it on a daily basis. In this entire experience, I hated that port the most. It felt so foreign and made me feel decrepit and old.

I also had to have a PET scan before chemo to see if the cancer had spread to any of my organs. Up to this point, I'd only had biopsies of my left breast.

This experience just kept getting more unbelievable. I wondered how many more surprises were down the road. It was all so new, I couldn't assimilate it all. As I looked through the scripts, I learned I would also need two kinds of anti-nausea medications, and steroids.

She even gave me a prescription for a medical cranium prosthesis, in layman's terms, a wig. It made sense to get the wig before I started losing my hair so I wouldn't have to run out quickly to buy one when I was in the throes of baldness, weakness, and nausea. There was no question as to whether I was going to lose my hair; it was just a matter of how quickly. Finally, Dr. S sent me on my way.

I was extremely eager to get started with chemo. Not that I wanted to, but just knowing about the aggressiveness of HER2+, I was naturally worried about it spreading quickly. The sooner I could get the chemo prerequisites out of the way, the sooner I could start the actual chemo and the sooner the cancer would stop growing. The ball had been put in my court. I had to schedule the echocardiogram and PET scan as soon as possible.

Receiving all this information from my breast surgeon and oncologist in one afternoon was overwhelming. I felt like all of my doctor appointments, tests, and procedures were like a snowball rolling down a hill, gaining speed. I needed a large monthly desk blotter just for keeping track of appointments related to my disease.

My husband had always been the sick one. Andy has high cholesterol, high blood pressure, chronic gout, GERD, debilitating and painful arthritis, disc pain, and sports and job-related injuries for which he has had several surgeries. He also suffers from allergies and asthma. He was Head Custodian for the White Plains City School District after having been a Custodian for many years. I always took *him* to his medical procedures and surgeries. Now, there was no question I had him beat.

We were thankful that when Andy retired early due to back and knee pain, he was able to take his medical coverage with him free of charge and only pay a minimal yearly amount to have me and the kids on his plan. Working for a school district, he had a really good plan. My medical fees for treatment, tests, and surgeries were never questioned. Thank God! I can't imagine how I would have handled the worry of not knowing if any part of my medical care would be covered while trying to get well.

Next on the blotter was the MRI biopsy, which was purported to be worse than the other two types of biopsies I'd had. At this point, though, it was really just another rung on the ladder of treatment. My scaredy-cat days were over by this time. I was facing chemo *and* surgery. I wasn't going to let this biopsy faze me.

Upon arrival, I was seated next to the MRI room to answer routine questions and get the IV set up for the contrast material. Then I was taken into the MRI room and positioned for the procedure. Unlike the other two biopsies, this one was longer and even more tedious.

Nothing seemed to go right. They had difficulty finding the area, and when they finally did, I think they missed numbing that spot because when the nurse jabbed me with whatever it was she used to obtain the sample, I screamed.

I thanked God I had said yes when they asked me if I wanted some Ativan in the IV to calm me down for the procedure. Even though I wasn't feeling any anxiety whatsoever, I thought it certainly couldn't hurt.

In spite of the noise of the MRI and the chaos of several people working around me, I slept through most of the procedure except for that jab of pain that woke me. Despite the three-ring circus, I'm thankful for the diligence of the technicians in locating the correct spot. Otherwise, it's possible they might not have found that there was, in fact, more cancer—ductal carcinoma in situ (DCIS).

Having a lumpectomy was no longer an option. The mastectomy was a must. I had cancer in three areas of my left breast, two in situ and one invasive.

The plan was to finish my chemo regimen and then have the left breast mastectomy. Dr. Z strongly recommended that I keep my right breast, even though I had the option of having a double mastectomy. He explained that ductal carcinoma couldn't spread to the other breast. If the cancer had been lobular, on the other hand, then I would definitely have needed the double mastectomy because that type of cancer could spread to the other breast.

In order for me to get cancer in my right breast, it would have to be a completely new, original cancer. My original cancer could metastasize to my brain or bones but not move into my other breast. I agreed that I should keep my other breast. It was extremely unlikely that I would get a second, original cancer since I was being treated for cancer at this point and would be for at least the next decade. My main worry was metastasis to my bones and brain.

The only thing left to decide was which type of reconstruction surgery I preferred. Dr. Z was not a plastic surgeon, but he gave me the names of several well-recommended plastic surgeons to call.

I'd never had any major surgery before. I couldn't even think about the upcoming mastectomy and reconstruction. It was beyond unnerving, but I didn't have to think about it until my long road of chemo was finished. For the time being, I pushed that inevitability completely out of my mind.

Since cancer and treatment is not the sort of thing I wanted to go through alone, and I needed all the prayers and encouragement I could get, I told my close friends. After a church service, I caught the attention of the pastor's wife, Liz, and told her about it. She suggested that I be prayed for right then and there. Without hesitation, I agreed.

Minutes later, she arranged for the pastor and several of the elders to gather in front of the sanctuary. Pastor Bobby anointed my head with oil, and he and the elders placed their hands on me while praying over me, according to James 5:14-15, which says, "Is anyone among you sick? Let him call for the elders of the church, and let them pray over him, anointing him with oil in the name of the Lord. And the prayer of faith will save the sick, and the Lord will raise him up. And if he has committed sins, he will be forgiven."

I didn't know if I should tell Sarah and David, who were 14 and 11 by this time, about my cancer. I knew Sarah could handle it, but I didn't want to tell David. As the younger child, he was a lot more attached to me than Sarah, but Andy didn't want me to keep it from either of them and insisted I tell them.

Initially, the shock of the news brought Sarah to tears. But after her first reaction, she was unemotional. Throughout the entire ordeal, she maintained that she wasn't worried because she knew everything was going to be okay. That was a good way of dealing with it, I thought. At times, though, she said it was unfair and questioned why God would let this happen to us.

David, on the other hand, took it hard. He was devastated by the whole thing. From the time he was told the news, he lived in a state of worry, no longer the boisterous, happy boy he had been.

Naturally, the diagnosis hit Andy the hardest. Heartbroken, he prayed for me almost continuously. There was nothing ritual about his prayers. With tears, he really poured out his heart to God. Although I might seem like the needy one in our marriage, Andy also has many deep needs that I fill in his life. God made us well-suited for each other.

My first chemo treatment was on June 25, 2012, and I started my new job in the Child Support Enforcement Unit (CSEU) at DSS, on July 2nd, seven days later. I was back at

DSS about five months after having been terminated from my position of Social Welfare Worker in the TA Intake Unit. I was glad to be in a department with good job security, especially in the midst of treatment.

Since I knew most of the people from TA, I was sure to see them walking in and out of the building or run into them in the elevator. They knew me and about my failure at TA. Now, I had to face them again. My plan had been to avoid them as much as possible.

But God had a unique plan for me at DSS. He was going to radically change my heart through my cancer experience and touch the lives of others, doing through me what I could never do on my own. My life would never be the same.

Chapter 20

HE IS THE MASTER POTTER

HEADING OFF TO MY FIRST CHEMO WITH MY HUSBAND, I hadn't the remotest idea what to expect. After taking the required five large steroid pills the evening before, I was up most of the night bouncing around the house, trying to occupy myself.

We had to be at the oncology place in Poughkeepsie by 8:30 a.m. Prior to this appointment, my prerequisite EKG had been done, and was normal, clearing me for Herceptin. The mandatory PET scan was also out of the way. Thank God, it revealed that the cancer hadn't spread to any of my organs. My power port had been surgically implanted in my chest. I was ready to go.

A nurse took me into the infusion room where about twelve recliner chairs filled the large room. The patients occupying the chairs were attached to IVs, which hung from tall metal poles on wheels. At the top of each pole, hooks held several bags of fluid.

I was told to pick a seat. After the blood work, blood pressure check, and all the preliminary rituals were finished, I was given an IV pole too. Then my nurse made her way over to me, barely managing to carry the armful of bags of fluid. One by one, she attached them to the various hooks atop my IV support.

"Wow, why so many bags?" I asked.

She explained that in addition to the Taxotere, Carboplatin, and Herceptin (TCH), I needed other drugs—Benadryl was so

I wouldn't have a fatal reaction to the toxicity of the chemo drugs (not a very comforting piece of information), anti-nausea medicine, and more steroids. There must have been eight bags stacked up for the day's infusion. Until then, I hadn't realized each treatment would take almost a full day. Hence, the lounge chairs.

The drip was finally started by 10:00 a.m. I wouldn't get out of there until 3:00 or 4:00 p.m., depending on how timely my nurse was in replacing my empty bags, while having other patients to take care of.

The only painful part of the day was when the nurse pressed the IV needle into my port through my skin. First, she sprayed the area with liquid ice, which really did make a difference, and I always asked for extra spray. Then, she had to press the needle into my chest just right. Even with the spray, that area was very sensitive.

On one occasion, I made the mistake of not using any spray. That was the day I got the attention of all the other patients. They turned their heads in sudden curiosity when they heard the loud *ow* come from the corner of the room by the window where I sat.

Once I was settled in, I felt a little like I was spending a day at the beach—lots of people surrounded me, I had my own little comfortable space, the music was good, and I had fun things to keep me occupied. I brought books, looked through magazines, or played games on my phone.

But mostly, I just lay there with a sense of gratitude that I was alive and with the inner hope that everything was going to be okay, which glimmered like the small flame of a candle that refused to go out.

My best friend, Marisa, whom I'd met years ago at church, took time off from work to take me to the remaining five chemo Mondays. The day was too long for Andy with his back problems. Marisa's the unique type of friend with whom I can be myself and share anything. Having her there with me was comforting, and we actually laughed a lot.

When I got home Monday evening and on into Tuesday, I felt okay because I had so many steroids in my system. I even felt good enough to drive myself back to the infusion room the next day for my Neulasta shot.

Even though I continued to take two kinds of anti-nausea medicine throughout the week, by Wednesday morning, the irrepressible, miserable nausea hit me. All I could manage to eat for the next three days was literally one slice of deli turkey and half a piece of toast twice a day. Thank God, Andy was there to bring that food upstairs because I was too weak and nauseated to do anything but lie in bed.

Every Wednesday, Thursday, and Friday following treatment, I did nothing but throw up, sleep, or just lie there like I'd been left for dead. By Sunday, a full week after chemo, I felt well enough to go to church. Monday, I went back to work for two weeks until the next cycle of chemo (every third Monday).

The timing of Andy's retirement in August of 2011 had been perfect. My chemo started in June of 2012. Had he not been there to take care of the kids during chemo and me after my surgery, I don't know how I would have managed. God arranged everything long before I even knew I was sick.

Totally out of the blue, the week before I started my new job, I received a canvass letter for a Case Manager position in Social Services. My name was still on the list for that exam I had taken years ago. That was the position I once wanted so desperately, but without giving it a second thought, I declined that interview.

Just starting chemo, I'd be lucky if I could handle my new clerical position let alone a high-stress, high-turnover job like Case Manager. I had wanted that type of job for all the wrong reasons, anyway.

I had started my new job at DSS the week immediately after my first chemo. I didn't have the next treatment until two weeks later. God's timing is always perfect.

My first day on my new job, I met with Tim, the head of our Personnel Department. I took the Case Manager canvass letter with me and told him I wasn't interested. I truly didn't regret not taking that opportunity for a promotion. I'd finally been humbled to where God wanted me to be.

About thirty-six of us comprised the Child Support Enforcement Unit (CSEU), including intake workers, enforcement workers, data entry staff, accounting staff, and six of us in clerical. God uniquely handpicked this job for me, and I was thankful and happy to be there.

Even though it was a clerical position, I decided to embrace my job as the important contribution to the unit it was. I enjoyed the work and the people.

A lady in the Risk Management department, who knew of my health situation, told me I couldn't have landed in a better job and department. DSS was known for going out of their way to accommodate employees who were going through family or health problems.

Additionally, my supervisor turned out to be empathetic to my situation. Only months before, her husband had gone through throat cancer. Very patiently, she trained me on processing family court petitions, filling in the templates for summonses and related documents, and serving the papers by regular mail to the parties involved.

The work was interesting, but one thing I learned quickly was that I couldn't have chemo on Monday and come to work that Wednesday or even Thursday. Further experience taught me that even on Friday, all bets were off.

For the duration of the six cycles, since I got chemo every third Monday, I was away from work my entire chemo week and then returned for the next two weeks—one week home, two weeks at work, and so on. Aside from my chemo week, I worked throughout the full course of treatment, which lasted about four-and-a-half months.

I also had to leave early every Monday for my weekly Herceptin infusions, which took about two hours. Fortunately, that gave me no short-term side effects, and I could work after that.

I knew I wasn't placed in this job by accident. God had a plan. I no longer defined myself by my job. My worth came from being a child of God and from the depths of His love for me.

He didn't create me so I could have a prestigious, high-paying job. This world is nothing but a vapor compared to eternity. He had a unique plan for my life that didn't involve me glorifying myself but rather for fulfilling His will for my life for His glory.

As the cycles of chemo continued, I felt weaker. I mistakenly believed that after the chemo week was done, I would have the next two weeks to recuperate, and my body would get back to normal. But the effects were cumulative, and true to the warnings, my hair fell out.

The first time I noticed, I was walking on the path around the park while waiting for my son to finish soccer practice. As I casually ran my fingers through my hair, I noticed clumps of hair in my hand. I've always had thick hair. I was able to go without a wig for a good while as my hair slowly thinned out.

Finally, my hair dwindled down to the point where Sarah said, "Mom, I think it's time for the wig." My wig somehow looked nicer than my real hair. I eventually did go totally bald. Andy would gently stroke my smooth pate every night as I fell asleep.

Toward the end of my chemo cycles, I slept for almost the entire day and night from Monday through Friday. By Saturday, after I'd hibernated like a bat in a dark cave for several days, Andy wanted me to get out of the house and move around. We would take the kids to the mall or run a few errands, but being out in public was difficult. Besieged by chemicals, my body was as close to dead as it could be.

Despite the rigorous treatment, the doctors couldn't be sure how effective it was, or if it was working at all. They were concerned that the cancer might have spread to my lymph nodes.

On one occasion, when I was having heart palpitations, my oncologist advised me to go to the hospital. My main worry was that the Herceptin might have adversely affected my heart. The chest x-ray showed that my heart was fine, but something suspicious appeared on my left axillary lymph node.

Also disconcerting was the fact that even though I was receiving chemo, my tumor markers were going up. Dr. S told me that with chemo, she would expect my markers to be going down, but she added that they could just be reacting to the havoc in my body caused by treatment, and that everything could be fine. Of course, it still had to be checked out.

About halfway through my chemo, I sat through an ultrasound-guided lymph node biopsy, biopsy number four, but thank God, that didn't show anything. Still, cancer spreading to my lymph nodes couldn't be ruled out. The only way to find out definitively would be during the mastectomy when Dr. Z would remove a sentinel lymph node for testing.

While limited to my bedroom one week out of three, cycle after cycle, I never would have gotten through it had I not had Jesus right there by my side. I felt His unmistakable, close presence. He never left me. During this unique time, I became aware of His perfect, all-sufficient love for me.

Throughout this physical malady and the darkness of not knowing if I would be healed or if this disease would kill me, the certainty of my dependency on Him was reassuring and all I needed. No matter what my fate, I knew my eternity was secure with Him. I know He is good and can be trusted because His will is always the best for me, no matter what it might be.

Much good has come out of this ordeal, for which I am thankful. I am closer to God in a way I've never known before. If getting closer to God were the only thing that came out of this trial, then it was more than worth going through.

If I were somehow given a choice to go back in time and not have cancer, I wouldn't have traded this experience. Knowing Him more is the most important outcome, but other blessings came out of this experience too.

God was doing something far more important for His glory than the temporary suffering of the moment. The Apostle Paul describes it this way, in two separate verses: "For our light affliction, which is but for a moment, is working for us a far more exceeding and eternal weight of glory" (2 Corinthians 4:17). "For I consider that the sufferings of this present time are not worthy to be compared with the glory which shall be revealed in us" (Romans 8:18).

God's Word is clear about how immeasurably He loves and cherishes His children. Through my cancer, I experienced God's intense love for me. I now see myself more the way He sees me, and love myself more the way He loves me.

I no longer need to prove anything to others as I did for so many years. According to Colossians 2:10, I am a complete person in Him. There is absolutely no one I desire to please but God. My only hope for a spiritually satisfying, purposeful life is to live for Him.

There is such futility in living for other people. Proverbs 29:25 states, "The fear of man brings a snare, but whoever trusts in the LORD shall be safe." I used to fear people, and I was certainly ensnared in that trap. Thank God, He has freed me from it. "Therefore if the Son makes you free, you shall be free indeed" (John 8:36).

Additionally, I realized that my harmful eating habits played a large part in getting cancer. At this point, I have come to a place where I eat healthfully and no longer run to food as an escape or to fill a void. First Corinthians 10:31 is a big help to me, because it reminds me to honor God in everything I do, including taking care of my body: "Therefore, whether you eat or drink, or whatever you do, do all to the glory of God."

As I became more dependent on God, I realized how weak I was, not because of having cancer, but because I'm human. We're all weak, but the wise ones recognize it. We can do nothing of any eternal value or spiritual significance in our own strength. Jesus says in John 15:5, "Without Me you can do nothing," At the same time, we "can do all things through Christ who strengthens [us]" (Philippians 4:13). The key in both those verses is being connected to Christ.

The Apostle Paul felt weak because of a "thorn in the flesh." He asked the Lord three times to remove it, but God answered, "My grace is sufficient for you, for My strength is made perfect in weakness" (2 Corinthians 12:9). If God's strength is made perfect in our weakness, clearly the weak person has the most power of all—God's power.

In fact, Paul goes on to say, "Therefore I take pleasure in infirmities, in reproaches, in needs, in persecutions, in distresses, for Christ's sake. For when I am weak, then I am strong" (2 Corinthians 12:10). It is all about being connected to and abiding in Jesus Christ for our strength: "Abide in Me, and I in you. As the branch cannot bear fruit of itself, unless it abides in the vine, neither can you, unless you abide in Me" (John 15:4).

Another benefit of this illness is that through this relatively brief time of treatment and surgery, Andy and I have become much closer. I knew Andy loved me, but this trial has shown me the great depths of his devotion.

Not only did he take care of the house and kids during my treatment, but he took care of me emotionally. He was always there to encourage me and make me laugh. I know God shows His enormous love for me through Andy. God is the One who put such a strong love for me in Andy's heart. Andy is one of God's most amazing and precious gifts to me.

In ways I can't fully understand, God has fashioned His mighty work in me, equipping me to live out His plan for my life. Ephesians 2:10 says, "For we are His workmanship, created in Christ Jesus for good works, which God prepared beforehand that we should walk in them."

Beyond what I could have hoped or imagined, God has opened up doors for me at work to touch lives for His glory.

Chapter 21

RESTORED

NOW THAT THE CHEMO NIGHTMARE WAS OVER, MY thoughts turned to the imminent mastectomy. I'd managed to suppress thoughts of that for the previous four-and-a-half months, but since it was scheduled at Vassar Hospital for November 6, only fifteen days away, I could no longer postpone thinking about it.

I'd never had any type of surgery, except when I had the port put into my chest, but that had been a quick, same-day procedure. I couldn't fathom that I was having an actual mastectomy, would be under anesthesia for some five hours, and have part of my body removed. This was big-time surgery. I could find no remedy for my fear of this.

Ten days after that, on November 16, I was scheduled to have another major surgery by a different doctor for the reconstruction. The mastectomy and reconstruction couldn't be done at the same time because if they discovered the cancer had spread to my lymph nodes, I would need radiation, which would damage the reconstructed breast. In that case, they would have to cancel the second surgery until after the completion of radiation. I needed fervent prayer for both surgeries.

When I arrived at the hospital, I was only a little nervous. As the hospital routine got underway, I was still only a bit uneasy, but as soon as they rolled me away on that gurney, I began to panic. My main fear was of being put under for several hours.

We had to make a few stops before reaching the operating room. First, I needed some kind of injection in my breast. No one had told me anything about that. As they wheeled me into a closet-like room off a hallway for the injection, the whole reality of the mastectomy hit me hard. I was petrified, and nothing could ease my heightened panic.

I didn't know the doctor. He was merely someone doing his part of my prep for the big event, but I could sense his empathy for me. I guess he thought I was nervous about what he was doing, but I was fine with getting an injection.

At some point during the roll-around time, a nurse sensed my anxiety and asked if she could pray with me. I couldn't imagine that even prayer could help the immensity of my worry, but I told her yes and that I was a Christian. It turned out she knew one of my neighbors and actually went to a weekly Bible study at her house. Immediately after she prayed, the fear lifted miraculously, and I felt fine. That she was there and offering to pray for me was no coincidence. I knew God was right there with me, arranging the help I needed. *Thank You, Lord, for sending her!*

Next, I was taken to get hooked up to the IV. Already feeling awkward about being pushed around in a horizontal position, I felt as though my attendant unnecessarily took the long route through many common areas of the hospital. As I was wheeled across the huge front lobby, I saw a vendor selling pocketbooks and jackets for a good cause. Then I was rolled past the gift shop and the cafeteria.

I couldn't believe this was the only route to the operating room. After all, I was only wearing a hospital gown. Feeling vulnerable, I noticed the awkward glances of visitors shuffling through the hallways. Their expressions seemed to convey their belief that I had something terminal. I prayed I wouldn't be parked and abandoned in a random hallway somewhere.

Finally hooked up to the IV, I answered a million times that, yes, my name was Barbara, and I was there for a mastectomy. The high caliber of care was outstanding, as were the kindness and expertise of all the medical staff I came in contact with.

Dr. Z, as usual, gentle and comforting, came by to see me. He seemed extremely confident and happy. That was reassuring.

At last, I was wheeled into the operating room. The scariest thing was being put under and having no control over it.

Then, like waking from a bad sleep, I knew it was all over. The whole thing had taken about five hours. Dr. Z came to see me in the recovery room. He was all smiles. Everything had gone well, and my lymph nodes were clean. *Praise the Lord!* My reconstruction surgery, set for ten days later, was a go.

When given my options for various reconstruction procedures, I knew I didn't want anything foreign in my body so I opted for using my own body tissue for reconstruction. After much research, I decided on the DIEP (deep inferior epigastric perforator) flap procedure.

My surgeon, Dr. G, was one of the best around and a pioneer in the DIEP flap procedure, still relatively new at the time. He had offices in Manhattan and Connecticut but had recently introduced this procedure at Vassar Hospital in Poughkeepsie, which was perfect since it was my preferred hospital, as well as the closest.

In simple terms, this technique involved using my stomach fatty tissue to form a reconstructed breast. Since this was a lengthy procedure, Dr. G. always worked with another physician to reduce the patient's amount of time in surgery. The entire operation took about five-and-a-half hours. Dr. G did an amazing job. Taking pride in his work, he was meticulous in every detail.

A four-day hospital stay was mandatory for this procedure. Dr. G stopped in to see me each day, monitoring my progress on a machine that tracked how well my blood vessels were connecting. If things didn't continue as planned, a trip back into surgery to fix the problem would be crucial—hence, my four-night stay in the hospital and Dr. G's forced vacation in Dutchess County's beautiful Mid-Hudson Valley.

My stomach had been cut straight across from hip to hip, so the first two days following surgery were a bit painful but not as bad as I'd expected. I only needed Motrin. I refused to take anything heavier, such as the morphine or other stuff they offered. I felt absolutely nothing in the breast area but was told that, in time, I would regain partial feeling as the nerves began to reconnect.

Having received the wonderful news about my clean lymph nodes and having come through my second surgery, I felt like the happiest person in that hospital wing. Knowing I was finally done with everything and the stomach pain would soon dissipate made this part of recovery a breeze.

When all was said and done, I'd had a tummy tuck, left breast reconstruction, right breast reduction, and lifts on both. Not a bad silver lining. And I couldn't have been more pleased with the results. I came out of this entire ordeal a new woman, having lost thirty pounds and gained a new tight stomach and the reduction and lifts I'd always wanted. I was more thankful, though, for the spiritual changes that had taken place in me.

After the four-day hospital stay, I went home on November 20 looking like a Christmas tree with all the bulbs dangling from the front of me. For several days, I sported six drain tubes, to siphon off the excess blood and fluid, hanging from my various incision sites. At the end of each tubular drain was a bulb-like pouch that collected the fluids. The whole thing was disgusting. Even more ghastly, the tubes had to be "milked" to squeeze out the fluids to prevent clogging and the bulbs emptied daily. Being squeamish, I couldn't do that.

If that weren't work-intensive enough, my wounds had to be cleaned and my dressings changed twice a day. That part sounds easy, but it was a laborious ritual. Greasy ointment had to be applied with a special kind of gauze, which had to be cut just right. Then, a different type of gauze and tape had to be applied over that.

Guess whose job it was to do the unimaginably grotesque milking and bandaging of my bloody tubes and wounds? Once again, my knight in shining armor, my Andy, rose to the occasion.

I wouldn't have blamed him if he'd bailed out. That was above and beyond the call of duty, but being the kind-hearted man that he is, he embraced the challenge, remembering his vows to love me "in sickness and in health." If I ever doubt Andy's love for me, I just have to remember the drain tubes.

Despite my wounds, I was in joyous spirits. Everything was finally over, and I couldn't have been happier that I didn't have to return to work until after the New Year, on January 3.

I had everything planned. With a pile of books and a Kindle my friend lent me loaded with several books she recommended, I relaxed and enjoyed one of my favorite passions, reading. Having nothing on my calendar and no work for almost a month and a half, I enjoyed a wonderful feeling of peace and relaxation.

After my recovery, I still had to have another PET scan, per Dr. S, my oncologist. Although the PET scan before chemo had shown nothing, the cancer could have spread during the chemo regimen. It was doubtful, but she wanted it ruled out.

The PET scan had to be the worst of all these surveillance procedures. The radiation it gave off was strong and the length of time uncomfortably positioned motionless in that tube was unpleasant. But thank the Lord, no cancer.

It was over. I was cancer-free. Thank You, Lord!

The fear of recurrence and metastasis will always loom over me, but it's a good fear. It forces me to take good care of myself and eat right.

I am still a cancer patient. I'll have to be on a medication protocol that carries its own set of debilitating side effects. For the next ten years, I have to take an estrogen blocker pill, Femara, every day and receive Lupron injections every three months.

Because I'm still not menopausal and my cancer was estrogen driven, the Lupron injections induce menopause by shutting down my ovaries to prevent any estrogen from being produced. The side effects of both these medications includes joint pain, bone density loss, easy bruising, high cholesterol, and fatigue. I will always suffer the irreversible intestinal neuropathy I sustained from the chemo, and my bone marrow will also never be the same.

Rather than being bitter, I accept these minor infirmities like a badge of honor. It's my conscious choice. Such maladies are a small price to pay for that brief time of affliction that not only destroyed the deadly cancer, but mysteriously purified the even more deadly dross from my heart and cleansed me spiritually in the process.

My body won't ever be the same, to be sure, but I've made many healthy lifestyle changes. Due to the bone density issue, I've begun to lift weights to help reverse that problem. God's been very gracious to me. I've had no joint pain whatsoever, and I've been managing the other symptoms. God willing, after ten years on these medications, *and* before I retire, I will be meds free.

I can rejoice in the fact that in my physical weaknesses and age-related ailments, I continue to grow spiritually. As Paul wrote in 2 Corinthians 4:16, I "do not lose heart. Even though [my] outward man is perishing, yet the inward man is being renewed day by day." What a hope-inspiring verse! In our weaker, elderly years, when we are forced to rely more on God for help, we can therefore grow more spiritually in the process.

After that wonderful and relaxing month and a half of recovery, I returned to work in January 2013 in the Child Support Enforcement Unit in a clerical capacity.

Regardless of my job duties, I immersed myself wholeheartedly into the work. Thankful to have a job and completely free from being defined by it, I did everything I could to be helpful in my clerical position, knowing that my worth comes from my heavenly Father's incredible love for me. That's all that matters, not how anyone looks at my position in life. My life's purpose is to do what God has called me to do, the way He has gifted and equipped me.

This world is nothing compared to eternity. I'm called to store up *eternal* treasures by testifying of what God has done for me, by speaking His truth, by committing loving actions in His name and by His power, and by leaving the results up to Him. The impact of those actions will last. Amassing money and gaining the esteem of others won't.

When the time was nearing for our supervisor, Maureen, to retire, most of us in CSEU-Clerical who were Senior Office Assistants (a grade eight), took the exam for her position, Principal Program Assistant, (a grade twelve).

A list was established just for our department (DSS) for Maureen's job. Five of us in the building on that list were interviewed. I was the only one in CSEU-Clerical who had scored high enough to be within reach for an interview.

A young woman in our building from Accounting got a ninety-five on the exam. I got a ninety. Since I worked in the unit and already knew most of the job, it would have made more sense to hire me, but initially, it went to her. I knew that God is the One in control. If God had wanted it for me, He would have worked it out. When she realized this was a dead-end job which offered her no growth opportunity, the woman put in her six months at CSEU-Clerical in order to obtain permanent status and then left for a lateral position in a department that provided ample room for advancement.

At that point, another woman from Administration in our building took the job, but after a week she decided she didn't like it. Finally, I was offered the job. I started in July 2016, four years after I started in July 2012.

God was working behind the scenes getting this job ready for me, and me ready for it. Two women in our clerical group would have given me a terrible time the moment I became their supervisor. Even when I came back from the interview, they began questioning me as to my ability to handle the job. They would have had zero respect for my authority.

Amazingly, during the first supervisor's six-month stay, one of them took an unplanned retirement, and the other one left. Additionally, during this time, two other people from our clerical group were promoted to Social Welfare Worker, a grade eleven, and moved to the Enforcement Worker positions within CSEU.

When I started as supervisor, I had several empty chairs to fill in my unit. As new people were hired, I was one of the interviewers along with our Director. I was fortunate to have several new staff members whom I chose, who weren't set in their ways, who appreciated their jobs, and whom I could train my way.

One of my primary responsibilities is to coordinate paternity testing with the clients, the lab, and Family Court. I also oversee the work of processing various child support petitions, court orders, personal services, and other related documents, making sure everything flows smoothly and correctly. Another major part of my job is supervising the eight employees in the Clerical and Data Entry Units.

I absolutely love this job. I love the diversity of responsibilities and all the contact I have with the staff in our unit, with Dutchess County Family Court, and with the staff at the DNA lab we use. My job is enjoyable and never boring. I love the challenge of problem solving, improving upon old procedures as things change, and helping develop the skill potential of my staff.

God gave me this job knowing I'd love it, and that with His help, I'd do well at it. I am so thankful to Him for this job, and I am committed to honoring Him in all aspects of it, especially in the way I communicate with and treat others.

It could be tempting to become prideful in my work, to try to impress others, to insist I'm right, or to even think I'm better than others. It all depends on whether I'm motivated to please and honor God, or if my selfish desires dominate my thinking. By His grace, I've been focusing on Him and working hard to help everyone administratively in the unit to His glory, as a witness of His goodness.

On any given day when unexpected work issues or personnel conflicts arise, my job can become difficult. I know I need God's help, not just every day but every moment. The only reason I have had such success on this job is because of prayer.

In fact, I was extremely nervous when I was first promoted, but God blessed me enormously, especially during my first year. When I had just started, my supervisor, the Director of Child Support, asked the four supervisors in the Child Support Unit to come up with money- and time-saving ideas for a special project. The other three "nominated" me to do the work, even though I was new to the job.

The four ideas I presented in our supervisors' meeting were well received, and the Director used two of them for the project. Early on, I made several improvements to procedures and work distribution. God has richly blessed me in helping me keep everything organized and running smoothly. Even when something got placed on my lap that was entirely new and I had no idea how to implement it, God saw me through with great success.

My supervisor, who has just recently retired, had often made a point of telling me what a great job I was doing and thanking me. Being nervous in the beginning, it was nice to hear that I was doing well. God was clearly blessing and helping me, but no one's approval, not even my supervisor's matters more than God's. The fact is God alone is in control of my job security. Gaining others' approval is an act of futility since it is usually conditional and fleeting, at best.

I prefer to focus on the things that count for eternity like helping someone accept the Lord rather than on temporary things like approval, money, and success. Working toward that goal includes sharing the Word of God with someone who needs to hear a certain verse, helping someone in need when God gives me opportunity, or just showing compassion for what someone is going through. Consistently kind behavior and a joyful demeanor at work can even touch someone's heart for God. An unfaltering spirit of joyfulness in a challenging work environment can speak volumes to an unbelieving observer.

God has blessed me in my job in ways I would never have imagined possible by opening doors for me to tell others about Him. Another Christian woman, Lisa, who also works in CSEU as a Court Specialist, and I have started a Bible study/prayer group at work during the morning break. What began with three people has grown to about eight regulars.

Several times a month we send an email reminder and invitation to attend to thirty-six people (so far) in our building. The emails, which either Lisa or I send out, include Scripture verses and an encouraging message of God's love.

During the morning break every day, we meet in the employee lounge and read a devotional for the day, including the Bible verses. We then discuss its application and relevance to our lives. With heads bowed and hands held, we conclude in prayer for those with urgent needs, for family and friends, and for the salvation of our co-workers in the building.

Many other people are also in the employee lounge as all this is going on. God is working powerfully in this Bible study/prayer group. Prayers are being answered, lives are being changed, and people are being saved.

How amazing it is that while I work a full-time, nine-to-five government job, I can still serve God in a powerful way! I actually have a platform to reach and influence more than thirty people for God by putting together a two-to-three paragraph email telling them about God's love and giving them the Gospel message.

I've often tended to compartmentalize the things I do like working, cleaning my house, free time, and time with the Lord. I especially separated working at my job and working for the Lord. Certainly, I didn't think those two activities could be combined. Now at work, I actually get to teach the Word of God at a daily Bible study and pray with a group of believers. Clearly, God can make anything happen.

On our unit, I have three Christian friends, two of whom go to my church. I can pray with them any time. Whenever I ask Lisa to pray for me, she will often stop what she's doing and pray out loud with me, as we hold hands. Most times, we even get on our knees, not caring what anyone might think. I am so thankful to God that I have a godly friend like Lisa.

When I decided to be thankful for my clerical job and honor God in it, He gave me a promotion into a supervisory, administrative position. I stopped caring about a high-status job but chose to simply do what God had called and gifted me to do—clerical work. His Word says, if you honor Him, He will honor you, and if you humble yourself before Him, He will in fact lift you up (see 1 Samuel 2:30b, James 4:10, 1 Peter 5:6).

The Bible is very clear that we are not here to pursue worldly success but to be a servant of God. Jesus, fully man and fully God, didn't come to earth to be served or to achieve a high position in this world, although He had the power to do so. He came to serve, heal, love others, and sacrifice His life so *our* sins could be forgiven.

Mark 10:45 tells us that "even the Son of Man did not come to be served, but to serve, and to give His life a ransom for many." And Philippians 2:5-8 says "Let this mind be in you which was also in Christ Jesus, who, being in the form of God, did not consider it robbery to be equal with God, but made Himself of no reputation, taking the form of a bondservant, and coming in the likeness of men. And being found in appearance as a man, He humbled Himself and became obedient to the point of death, even the death of the cross." *He* is our example.

I hope my story has been a blessing to you. Having a personal relationship with God, through His Son, Jesus Christ, by the power of the Holy Spirt, is the highest calling and most wonderful experience you can have. Whether or not you have a personal relationship with God, the truth is He loves you immeasurably. In Jeremiah 31:3, God says to you and me, "I have loved you with an everlasting love; therefore with lovingkindness I have drawn you."

Because of my own experience, I can say that no matter how far away from Him you might be or what unthinkable things you may have done, and no matter how impossible you believe your problems and pain to be, God is bigger and can do more than you can ever hope or imagine.

In Revelation 3:20, the risen Christ says, "Behold, I stand at the door and knock. If anyone hears My voice and opens the door, I will come in to him and dine with him, and he with Me." Jesus is speaking at the door of your heart. He is knocking because He won't force His way in. It has to be your choice to open the door.

God beckons to you, saying, "Call to Me, and I will answer you, and show you great and mighty things, which you do not know" (Jeremiah 33:3). Now is the time. Tomorrow is not guaranteed. Later might be too late. In 2 Corinthians 6:2, the Apostle Paul warns, "Behold, now is the accepted time; behold, now is the day of salvation," echoing the Old Testament Prophet Isaiah, who wrote, "Seek the LORD while He may be found. Call upon Him while He is near" (Isaiah 55:6).

Salvation is beautifully simple.

First, you must admit that you are a sinner. "For all have sinned and fall short of the glory of God" (Romans 3:23). As I described in Chapter 13, no one is good enough to go to heaven on his own merit. No matter how much good we do, we still fall short.

Second, you must realize that the penalty for sin is death, according to Romans 6:23: "The wages of sin is death, but the gift of God is eternal life in Jesus Christ our Lord." Just as there are wages for good work, there is punishment for wrongdoing. The penalty for sin is eternal death in a place called hell, the Lake of Fire (see Revelation 20:14-15). God doesn't send people to hell. By rejecting or neglecting God's provision for salvation through His Son, Jesus, we send ourselves.

Third, you must recognize that Jesus Christ died, was buried, and rose again for you. "If you confess with your mouth the Lord Jesus and believe in your heart that God has raised Him from the dead, you will be saved" (Romans 10:9).

Fourth, you must trust Christ alone as your Savior. "For whoever calls on the name of the Lord shall be saved" (Romans 10:13). Referring to the name of Jesus Christ, the Apostle Peter declared, "Nor is there salvation in any other, for there is no other name under heaven given among men by which we must be saved" (Acts 4:12). Eternal life is a gift purchased by the blood of Jesus shed on the cross and given freely to all who call upon Him in faith. The Lord Jesus Christ will save anyone who believes on Him.

There is no magic formula or specific words. What matters to God is the sincerity of your heart. Here is a simple prayer that you can pray right now, or you can say your own, as long as you are genuinely seeking God and His will for your life:

> God, I am a sinner. Please forgive me. Thank You for sending Your Son, Jesus, to die on the cross for my sins so I can be with You for all eternity. I give up trying to do things on my own. I need You, and I make You Lord of my life. Thank You for Your free gift of salvation to me. In Jesus' name, Amen.

If you said that prayer sincerely or used your own words—congratulations! God is faithful to come into your life and lovingly pick up the pieces, heal you, grow you, and empower you to live for His glory.

Repentance of sin means to completely turn your back on sin and pursue God's righteousness instead. You can do this now because according to 2 Corinthians 5:17, you are a new creation in Christ: "Therefore, if anyone is in Christ, he is a new creation; old things have passed away; behold, all things have become new."

The key to effective Christian living is to abide in Jesus. Just as a branch must be connected to a vine to bear fruit, we must stay connected to Him and surrender every part of our life to Him in order to grow spiritually. The following five activities will serve you well, as they do me, in your walk with Jesus to help you abide in Him.

1. Read the Bible every day.
2. Pray daily.
3. Fellowship—Stay in contact with other believers through regular church attendance, Bible study groups, and Christian social gatherings.
4. Minister to the needs of others—With the love and comfort God has imparted to us in our pain, we are distinctively prepared to show others that same compassion and help. We become beacons of love and healing to others. As the Apostle Paul said of his sufferings,

> "Blessed be the God and Father of our Lord Jesus Christ, the Father of mercies and God of all comfort, who comforts us in all our tribulation, that we may be able to comfort those who are in any trouble, with the comfort with which we ourselves are comforted by God" (2 Corinthians 1:3, 4).

5. Witness—love unbelievers and help them to know God by sharing your testimony of what God has done for you and telling them the salvation message.

God created each of us with a plan in mind—a unique plan for each individual. God has promised in His Word, "For I know the thoughts that I think toward you, says the LORD, thoughts of peace and not of evil, to give you a future and a hope" (Jeremiah 29:11).

Immediately upon giving our lives to God, He begins to change us to be the new creations He intends us to be. In our redeemed life, God can use every part of our past for His glory and purpose, and for our good (Ephesians 2:10). Our changed life becomes the display of His power to a watching world. We are His masterpieces, His work of art. Others will see the difference in us and be drawn to God because of our testimony to His power.

I pray you will seek more of God in your life, experience His limitless power to serve Him mightily, and victoriously live out His wonderful plan for your life as the new creation He has destined you to be!

For further information about

Barbara Kabot-Vena

&

A New Creation Ministry

Please visit: *http://BarbaraKabot-Vena.blogspot.com/*

CPSIA information can be obtained
at www.ICGtesting.com
Printed in the USA
BVHW071311100619
550590BV00006B/399/P

9 781545 666968